Endorsements for Cross Words

"Some people think, speak and read in sentences. Others use single words to express themselves. In their busy world, a 'Hi' & 'Bye Now' suffices for those on the run.

But both full sentences and single words appropriately convey our message. Nick Furey skillfully introduces us to Bible words in the form of acronyms. I am sure that we will find them helpful as we hurry through life. Use them for personal profit and real pleasure."

Pastor Ray Anderson, too old to retire!

"This book is a "must read" for new Christians, though it can benefit all believers. Through simple acronyms, this unique book can help you painlessly hide God's Word in your heart. The 52 acronyms help link basic Christian beliefs directly to Scripture, making it a great devotional tool. It allows you to meditate on one word a week for an entire year, or you can utilize the book's suggested 13-week plan. Whatever you choose, you won't be disappointed."

Pastor Bob Aspling
Crown Christian Family Church
Duluth, MN

"I am having a lot of fun picking out different acronyms and am amazed on how relevant they are in my everyday life. For instance, **DOUBT** – **D**epending **O**n **U**nderstanding **B**efore **T**rusting…How many times do I wish I would learn to trust instead of DOUBT?

C.J.
A relatively new "born again" Christian

Cross Words

Renewing your mind
with Acronyms of HOPE

<u>72</u> of the acronyms are original inspirations, as, after much research, I have not found them to be used anywhere else. This book and all its contents direct results of listening to God's voice and direction. All people and situations have been used with permission.

All Scriptures are taken from (NIV) Zondervan CD-ROM

Nick Furey
A Christian Voice Publishing
Duluth, MN

©Copyright 2006, Nick Furey
All rights reserved.

No part of this book may be reprinted, stored in a retrieval system, or transmitted by any means, electronic, mechanical, photocopying, recording, or otherwise, without permission from the author. However, Pastors, teachers, missionaries, speakers, and people in general may use the acronyms as tools to strengthen their message without permission; just acknowledge the source.

Simple Faithworks
Nick Furey
simplefaithworks.com

Publisher
A Christian Voice Publishing
Suite 103
102 South 29th Ave. West
Duluth, MN 55806
218-722-3299
achristianvoicepublishing.com

Cover Design:
Nick Furey/Amy Poster
A Christian Voice

Dedication

Sam, Joseph, and Lydia – I love you!

I dedicate this book to all the people who are living in despair – There is HOPE!

PREFACE

If you are traveling down the road and one of your tires go flat, think of the three tools you would need to change the tire: a jack, a crossbar (or lug wrench), and of course a spare tire. If you only had a screwdriver, it would not be of much use and the job could not be done. Most car manufacturers provide these three tools, but most of the time they are hidden in some of the most unlikely places. With the proper tools, you can change your tire and get on your way. I believe these word tools can help you change your life. The jack and crossbar do not actually change the tire, the person does. We cannot change anyone; we need to be the tools to help them to see the problem areas in their life and change.

Note: I have purposefully cited the Scripture verses in their entirety, rather than just listing the book and verse number. I hope that having a little taste of the words of Scripture will give you a desire to read more of what they say in and around the verse that is quoted and other areas that will help you. If you don't have a bible, I encourage you to get one. If you have one, read it! It is the manual to survive life.

I also know that some of the acronyms either sound "corny" or misused. For instance, in the acronym, **AWE** -the word Everyday should be separated as Every Day; however, putting them together brings out the meaning of a particular acronym. I ask you to bear with me and understand the meaning that God wants for your life.

Acronyms are, as defined in Merriam-Webster Dictionary:

ac•ro•nym \"a-krō-'nim\ *n* : a word (as *radar*) formed from the initial letter or letters of each of the successive parts or major parts of a compound term

(c)2000 Zane Publishing, Inc. and Merriam-Webster, Incorporated. All rights reserved.

I have written this book to encourage others to understand that our faith in God is a simple concept. The acronyms may enlighten your understanding of common words we use, and I pray they become like "pop-ups" in your mind whenever you say one of them. I have seen the light bulb of understanding go off in people's minds as they have heard the meaning of these words.

I asked God to give me a "mission statement" or purpose for this book and my ministry, and He directed me to the following Scripture:

Colossians 2:2-6;

> *2 <u>My purpose is that they may be encouraged in heart and united in love, so that they may have the full riches of complete understanding, in order that they may know the mystery of God, namely, Christ,</u> 3 <u>in whom are hidden all the treasures of wisdom and knowledge.</u> 4 I tell you this so that no one may deceive you by fine-sounding arguments. 5 For though I am absent from you in body, I am present with you in spirit and delight to see how orderly you are and how firm your faith in Christ is.*

I hope you find solace in the words of this book, but moreover, I want the words of Scripture to nourish and refresh you.

TABLE OF CONTENTS

INTRODUCTION TO FAITH   page 11
WEEK 1 ----- HOME –
    What makes your home a haven?
- **HOME**..page 16
- **MOM**..page 19
- **DAD**...page 22
- **CHILD**...page 24

WEEK 2 ---- FAITH – Do you fully trust Him?
- **FAITH**..page 28
- **HOPE**...page 31
- **LOVE**...page 35
- **PRAY**...page 41

WEEK 3 ---- GOD ---Who do you say that I am?
- **GOD**...page 46
- **JESUS**..page 48
- **LORD**..page 50
- **AWE**..page 52

WEEK 4 ---- CROSS – Do you want to be rescued?
- **CROSS**...page 56
- **SAVED**..page 61
- **PEACE**..page 65
- **ROCK**..page 68

WEEK 5 ---- GROW –What does it take to GROW in the Lord?
- **GROW**...page 72
- **PURE**...page 75
- **CHOICE**..page 78
- **HEAR**..page 80

WEEK 6 ----FEAR –What prevents you from knowing God?
- **FEAR**...page 84
- **DOUBT**...page 88
- **GUILT**...page 90
- **SHAME**...page 94

WEEK 7 ---- SIN – Has SIN mastered you?
- **SIN**.. page 98
- **STOP**.. page 101
- **EVIL**... page 103
- **LUST**... page 108

WEEK 8 ---- HOLY – Is your life set apart for God?
- **HOLY**.. page 116
- **OBEY**.. page 118
- **WORD**.. page 121
- **ZEAL**.. page 125

WEEK 9 ---- CARE –
How do you show people that they are loved?
- **CARE**.. page 128
- **SMILE**... page 132
- **GIVE**... page 134
- **HUG**... page 139

WEEK 10 ---- FORGIVE –
Are you willing to let go and let God?
- **PAST**... page 142
- **PRIDE**... page 145
- **SORRY**.. page 148
- **FORGIVE**.. page 150

WEEK 11 ---- TRUTH – What is Truth?
- **TRUTH**.. page 156
- **TRUST**.. page 159
- **WAY**... page 165
- **PRAISE**... page 167

WEEK 12 ---- CHURCH – What purpose does it serve?
- **CHURCH**.. page 172
- **ALTAR**.. page 175
- **PASTOR**... page 180
- **RNR** (not an original)..................... page 183

WEEK 13 ---- ANGELS – Who's looking out for you?
        ANGELS.. page 188
        ACTS... page 190
        BRAVE... page 193
        MUSIC... page 196

OTHER INSPIRED WORDS..................... page 199

CONCLUSION... page 201

BIBLIOGRAPHY....................................... page 209

ILLUSTRATION…………………….….. page 217

ABOUT THE AUTHOR........................... page 219

ACKNOWLEDGEMENTS....................... page 220

Cross Words -- Introduction

INTRODUCTION TO FAITH

In my life I have faced a lot of ups and downs, but the downs are what make the ups that much more enjoyable. I know that all the pain and hardship I have faced up to now have brought me to the point where I had to cry out God, as Jabez did, "God, please bless me, I want to hear your voice. I want others to know you, and I am willing to be an instrument of your grace and compassion."

1 Chronicles 4:9-10

> *ICH 4:9 Jabez was more honorable than his brothers. His mother had named him Jabez, saying, "I gave birth to him in pain." 10 Jabez cried out to the God of Israel, "Oh, that you would bless me and enlarge my territory! Let your hand be with me, and keep me from harm so that I will be free from pain." And God granted his request.*

God answered Jabez' prayer, and mine. He has been more than gracious to me since I asked Him to speak to me. This introduction is an understanding on how the Lord began to answer my prayer and speak to me through the acronyms. And this journey began in 2000 through a simple prayer and the hearts of some children.

Cross Words -- Introduction

One morning as I was teaching the Children's Sunday Service at my church, I told the children about Faith. I was using the teaching tool of the "faith catch", where you have them close their eyes and fall back into your arms, trusting that you will catch them. Inevitably they would wobble or try to catch themselves. I explained that that is just how we are with God; we don't really trust Him so we feel as though we need to catch ourselves.

For the ones that did trust me, they found it comforting to know that I would never drop them. My oldest son, Sam, however, jumped into line, and fell back when I was still talking to the other kids. Needless to say, he was a bit surprised that he had to catch himself. Sometimes we do things expecting God to just be there to catch us, even when we do foolish things. Not that God can't catch us, but like my son, we learn a very important lesson: Trust God, but don't put Him to the test.

I also shared with the children how Christ said; "If you only had faith the size of a mustard seed, you could say to this mountain, 'Be lifted up and thrown into the sea!' and it would." Well, I showed the children a mustard seed. They were astonished at how incredibly small it was! So was I! And yet, that mustard seed, as small as it is, will grow into a large tree, providing shelter for many birds and shade for people.

Matthew 13:31-32

> [31] *He told them another parable: "The kingdom of heaven is like a mustard seed, which a man took and planted in his field.* [32] *Though it is the smallest of all your seeds, yet when it grows, it is the largest of garden plants and becomes a tree, so that the birds of the air come and perch in its branches."*

I explained how Jesus spoke of having faith as a little child. When I told my daughter, Lydia, "I am going to lasso the moon and bring it home for you", she believed that it would happen, and still asks me when I am going to bring it home for her!

When I tell my son Joseph, that Jesus is coming back very soon, he will frequently ask me how soon, as if it will happen tomorrow. And if I tell my children that Jesus loves each and every one of them, they believe it! Not so much because I said so, rather, because they have faith that if the Bible says that it is true, then it must be true.

Jesus said in:

Cross Words -- Introduction

Matthew 18:3-4

> *³ And he said: "I tell you the truth, unless you change and become like little children, you will never enter the kingdom of heaven. ⁴ Therefore, whoever humbles himself like this child is the greatest in the kingdom of heaven."*

After I had spent time with the class, I went home, and, like a light-bulb, the acronym F.A.I.T.H came to me as Find Assurance In Trusting Him. As a funeral director, I had the opportunity to talk with numerous different clergy, and they encouraged me to put my acronyms into a book. When I became available to God, the acronyms started coming in like a floodgate being opened up.

NOTE **

This book is designed to be a 13-week study, reading only 4 Acronym chapters a week - meditating and applying their meaning to your life in that week and for the rest of your life.

- **Examine the word, its acronym, and most of all the Word of God that coincides with it.**

- **Ask yourself the study questions**

- **Reflect on the prayer. The prayer is to give you a start in praying to God. Begin to talk with Him daily.**

- **You will truly find yourself with a more fulfilling relationship with God.**

Week 1

__HOME__

What makes your home a haven?

HOME – **H**aven **O**f **M**y **E**xistence

MOM – **M**ade **O**f **M**iracles

DAD – **D**edicated **A**nd **D**evoted

CHILD – **C**hrist **H**as **I**nnocent **L**ittle **D**isciples

Cross Words – Week 1 - HOME

HOME
Haven Of My Existence

2 Peter 3:13;
"But in keeping with his promise we are looking forward to a new heaven and a new earth, the home of righteousness."

A Haven is defined as "a safe sanctuary where one can find peace". Our **HOME** is to be a safe haven for all who enter it. We must consider how we can accomplish this. What types of movies, games, books, or magazines do we bring into our home? What types of conversations do we have? Are we only using kind words to those who are there? No matter where you live, whether it is a 5 bedroom house or a little shack, we can make it a home if we cause it to be a haven where we exist.

And what about the people who are **HOME**less? What ways can we help provide a Haven for them? We can get so caught up in having a nice house that we can call home that we can often forget that there are people that have no place call **HOME**, and this is not necessarily their fault. For instance, consider the people hit by Hurricane Katrina; was it their fault

Cross Words – Week 1 - HOME

that their homes were ruined leaving them **HOME**less?

Keep in mind, the only real way to make our house a **HOME** is to have the Lord the Lord of it. He is the One who provides direction and peace for our lives. Our real goal is to prepare those who enter our **HOME** for their eternal **HOME** that is being prepared for them in Heaven.

At most, we can hope to live a little more than 100 years here, and in heaven we will live forever. Consider the part of the song "Amazing Grace" that states, *"When we've been there ten thousand years, bright shining as the sun…"* But this world and all the wonderful things in it is not our home. We can also make a real home for Jesus here, within our hearts. Would Jesus find your heart to be a haven?

- ❖ Take time this week to make a Haven of your Home.
- ❖ What can you do to ensure that your house is a **HOME**, for you and others?

Cross Words – Week 1 - HOME

PRAYER

Father, I thank you that have provided me with a HOME. I pray that I will be able to make it a Haven for my family and others. Help me to see those who have no place to call HOME and help them the best that I can. Most of all, I pray that my heart can be a suitable HOME for Jesus to abide. Bless this HOME Lord and keep us safe, that we might serve you. Amen.

Cross Words – Week 1 - MOM

MOM

Made Of Miracles

John 2: 5, 11;

> [5] *His <u>mother</u> said to the servants, "Do whatever he tells you."....* [11]*This, is the first of his <u>Miraculous</u> signs, Jesus performed at Cana in Galilee. He thus revealed his glory, and his disciples put their faith in him,"*

My mother thought I was using the word "Maid", instead of "Made"; I told her that I appreciated everything she has done for me and yet I do not want her to ever be treated as a maid. Moms are really the unsung heroes of life; they are the only ones who can actually bring us into the world. What an amazing gift, to go through nine months of all sorts of body changes, aches, and pains, in order to bring a new life into this world. That's love!

And to the single moms that have to bear the challenge alone, God is a faithful Father – the Father of the fatherless, the strength when you feel weak, the sustainer of all your needs. He loves you as no one could ever do.

Cross Words – Week 1 - MOM

My children's MOM has always been a great source of strength to them. The pain she went through to bear each child was more than a miracle. I remember being in tears as they were born; excited for a new child, yet so proud of her. She cares for each of them dearly.

The bond between a mother and a child is such an amazing miracle. Even the worst of mothers still longs for a close bond with their child. Though a child may be angry with their mother for a while, there is always that desire to have a good relationship with the one who gave them life.

- ❖ If you are a **MOM**, what Miracles are you doing for your children?

- ❖ Scripture says, "Though a mother should forsake her child, I will never abandon you"; I urge you to love your children no matter what.

- ❖ There are resources available to help you become the MOM God intended you to be – like MOPS (Mothers Of PreschoolerS – MOPS.org), or ask your church if they have groups for MOMs.

- ❖ Take a moment to thank your mom; send her a card, call her, just remember her, or stop by to let her know you appreciate her.

Cross Words – Week 1 - MOM

PRAYER

Father, I thank you that you have provided me with a wonderful MOM. She gave me life, and for that Miracle alone, I am grateful. I pray for her in all that she does. I am thankful, Jesus, that your own mother was willing to be a servant of God and bring you – the greatest Miracle, into this world. Lord, there are many MOMs that are having to bear the responsibility of raising her children alone; please give them the strength and hope they need. Amen.

Cross Words – Week 1 - DAD

<u>DAD</u>

Dedicated **A**nd **D**evoted

Mark 14:36

> *[36] "Abba, Father," he said, "everything is possible for you. Take this cup from me. Yet not what I will, but what you will."*

A song that clearly explains how fathers have an awesome responsibility to lead their children to know who God is:

"I want to be just like you, because he wants to be like me."
By Phillips, Craig, and Dean (used with permission)

In this song, they mention of how the little boy watches everything that his daddy does and wants to someday be like him. The dad realizes that he has an awesome responsibility to be a holy example to his boy and he cannot do it all alone, he needs the help of his Heavenly Father. Are you spending time with your Heavenly Father learning how to be a better DAD?

Dedicated and Devoted would seem to mean the same thing, however, Dedicated refers to how much a dad is willing to do things for his children (in his mind), and Devoted refers to how much he actually feels like doing it (in his heart). For instance,

Cross Words – Week 1 - DAD

a dad could go to every single game that his child is involved in, but never really show the enthusiasm and encouragement to his child.

I love being a DAD, and find it such a challenge and a joy to have this privilege. I am thankful that I have a great DAD that has supported and helped me over the years, and a Heavenly Father (Dad) that has loved me beyond measure.

- ❖ Do you have a DAD in your life now?
    - ○ --If not, do you realize we have a Heavenly Father (DAD) that will never leave or forsake you, and "He is a Father to the Fatherless". - Psalm 68:5

- ❖ If you are a DAD, be sure to be both Dedicated and Devoted to your children, never give up on them.

- ❖ Anyone can be a father; it takes someone very special to be a DAD.

- ❖ What steps are you willing to take to become a better DAD?

PRAYER

Father, I am grateful that you are such a loving DAD, caring so much for me that you give me what I need and correct me when necessary. Help all the DADs out there to care about their children the way you care about them. Amen.

Cross Words – Week 1 - CHILD

CHILD

Christ Has Innocent Little Disciples

Matthew 18:2-5;

> *² He called a little child and had him stand among them. ³ And he said: "I tell you the truth, unless you change and become like little children, you will never enter the kingdom of heaven. ⁴ Therefore, whoever humbles himself like this child is the greatest in the kingdom of heaven. ⁵ "And whoever welcomes a little child like this in my name welcomes me."*

That's right; children are Christ's **Innocent** little disciples. That means they have a purpose and place in God's work. So, just because you are young doesn't mean that God cannot use you. In truth, it means He may be able to use you more because of your childlike faith.

Consider the life of David… though a mere shepherd boy, and the youngest of the family, he was not only the one who killed the giant, Goliath, but also the one whom God had selected to be king! Not based on size or experience, rather, based on having the heart of God.

Cross Words – Week 1 - CHILD

A warning to all adults – Scripture specifically states the punishment for anyone who harms a little child or causes him to sin!

Matthew 18: 6;

> *"But if anyone causes one of these little ones who believes in Me to sin, it would be better for him to have a large millstone hung around his neck and to be drowned in the depths of the sea."*

This sounds strong and overbearing, but that is just how serious the matter is! God cares that much about the innocence of His little disciples.

Parents want to be able to trust their children when they are not in their care. When mom or dad says "no", accept it! When they say get home by a certain time, they want to be able to trust their child to obey them. Not for dominance, but for the sense of care, responsibility, and most of all, love.

- ❖ Are you a parent/teacher? What ways can you encourage and help Christ's Innocent Little Disciples?

Cross Words – Week 1 - CHILD

- ❖ As a CHILD, you need to continually desire to learn more about Christ and His purpose for you. Remember God can use you.

- ❖ Remember, we are all a CHILD of God when we accept Jesus into our heart.

PRAYER

Father, I thank you that I can call you my Father. I am proud to be your CHILD. Help me to be the CHILD that you can be proud of. Bless and protect all your Little Disciples in this world. Amen.

Week 2

FAITH

Do you fully trust Him?

FAITH – **F**ind **A**ssurance **I**n **T**rusting **H**im

HOPE – **H**ave **O**nly **P**ositive **E**xpectations

LOVE – **L**et **O**ur **V**alues **E**ndure

PRAY – **P**ower **R**esounds **A**round **Y**ou

Cross Words – Week 2 - FAITH

<u>FAITH</u>

Find Assurance In Trusting Him

Hebrews 11:1,
> *"Now faith is being sure of what we hope for and certain of what we do not see."*

We have complicated a very simple concept. We have turned faith into a trigonometry type of concept, when it should be just plain addition: 1 (Me -Trusting Jesus) + 1 (Jesus - who Saved me) = 2 gether forever in Paradise.

Ephesians 2:8;
> *"We are saved by grace, through faith, and not of works, otherwise men would boast."*

It is important to remember that we are **<u>saved by grace</u>**. Faith assists us in accepting and understanding our salvation, but we also are to show that by helping others so they too might trust Jesus and be saved.

Trust is such an important factor to influence our walk with

Cross Words – Week 2 - FAITH

Jesus. It also can be the very reason we are stumbling day-to-day, because of our lack of faith to trust Him with everything. Lack of faith is mostly why many people are so miserable.

Matthew 13:58;
> *"And he did not do many miracles there because of their lack of faith."*

Mark 6:4-6;
> [4] *Jesus said to them, "Only in his hometown, among his relatives and in his own house is a prophet without honor."* [5] *He could not do any miracles there, except lay his hands on a few sick people and heal them.* [6] *And he was amazed at their lack of faith.*

Jesus was very disappointed in the lack of faith of the people in His hometown. In fact, it hindered His ministry. Christ's power thrives on our faith, yet He was unable to do any miracles, due to their lack of faith.

Consider the parable that Jesus used to describe faith.

Matthew 7:24-27;
> [24] *"Therefore everyone who hears these words of mine and puts them into practice is like a wise man who built his house on the rock.* [25] *The rain came down, the streams rose, and the winds blew and beat against that house; yet it did not fall, because it had its foundation on the rock.* [26]

Cross Words – Week 2 - FAITH

> *But everyone who hears these words of mine and does not put them into practice is like a foolish man who built his house on sand. ^{27} The rain came down, the streams rose, and the winds blew and beat against that house, and it fell with a great crash."*

The disciples asked Jesus to increase their FAITH, His response was always, "Trust me."

- ❖ Do you Trust in Jesus? How much?
- ❖ Where is **_your faith_** at this time in your life?
- ❖ Is your faith built on the solid rock, or are you relying on your own strength and understanding on a foundation of sand.
- ❖ Are there areas of your faith that need strengthening?
- ❖ Are you willing to leave your house on sand, just to start over on a house built on a solid rock?

PRAYER

Father, I put my FAITH in you. I know that as I TRUST you, I will grow and understand your wonderful plan for my life. Though I cannot see you now, I know that I will see you face to face when I am finally before your throne. Help me to put FAITH in action by helping those around me. Amen

Cross Words – Week 2 - HOPE

<u>HOPE</u>

Have Only Positive Expectations

Job 11:18;

> [18] *You will be secure, because there is <u>hope</u>; you will look about you and take your rest in safety.*

One of my favorite quotes is from Winston Churchill's address to the soldiers during World War II, "Never, never, never, give up!" With hope, there is no reason to give up. We feel that there is still a chance that things will work out.

Hope is a more than just a feeling; it is an inner desire.

Leave behind a living legacy. Do the right thing each day and never give up on fulfilling your dreams. Remember, legacies can be both good and bad. Sure, you can be remembered by all the bad things you do, but do you really want to pass that along to the next generation?

Consider then, each day, how what you do will affect the lives of your family, friends, and others. Your children are one of the greatest legacies you can leave behind. You must Have

Cross Words – Week 2 - HOPE

Only Positive Expectations, and someone to help you. It is up to you, though, to change your ways.

A large ship was traveling on the Great Lakes on a foggy, windy, stormy day. The captain listened to his radio, "Great Lakes ship, please move 25 degrees north out of my way."
The ship's captain was very arrogant and figured he was much too proud and important to move, so he said, "This is the Great Lakes ship. No, you move!"
The voice came back on the radio, "Great Lakes ship, you must move out of my way immediately!"
The angered captain responded, "I am a large, important ship, you move!"
Finally, the voice came back on the radio stating, "Great Lakes ship, this is the Lighthouse, I must insist you move or you'll crash on the rocks!"

Once we part with the bad things in our life, we must then fill the void with positive energies. One way to do this is by being a great husband, wife, mother, father, child, worker, etc.

Give of yourself to your family and friends and you will have a

Cross Words – Week 2 - HOPE

lasting legacy.

There is a saying that I have heard over the years, "Plan for the worst, but hope for the best." That is another way of killing hope, giving up on it before you give it a chance. The planning involves what we can do now, with full intention that only the negative will happen. leaving the catcher to hope. What if we changed that around to say "Plan, and hope for the best."? I know what people really mean by that old saying; you should be prepared for any adversity that may come in your path, but always hope that you can get through it; but why must we use that negative "the worst" at all.

If you Have Only Low Expectations, you are nothing more than living in a HOLE! Get up out of there and start thinking Positive.

Now the real work takes place; we must put our hopes and dreams into action. Hope, then, is more than just wishing. It is putting our expectations (wishes and desires) into action, with the decision that we will settle for nothing less than a Positive outcome.

Cross Words – Week 2 - HOPE

- ❖ Are there days you feel like there is no HOPE?
- ❖ Are you willing to Have Only Positive Expectations in order get through each day?
- ❖ Have you found the true source of HOPE – Jesus?
- ❖ What negatives in your life hold you back from being your best.
- ❖ Remember ..... Never, never, never give up.

<u>Prayer</u>

Father, thank you for sending Jesus to be our source of HOPE. There are days in my life where I feel like there is so much despair that I need you to remind me of the Positive Expectations that you have of me. I put my HOPE in you. Amen.

Cross Words – Week 2 - LOVE

LOVE
Let Our Values Endure

John 3:16;

> *"For God so loved the world that he gave his one and only Son, that whoever believes in him shall not perish but have eternal life.*

John 3:16 (my amplified version);

> *"It was out of God's great Love for the entire world, which He created, that He gave up His one, and only, Perfect Son, so that whosoever (Black, White, Yellow, or Red skinned people from wherever -Asia, Europe, Africa, the Americas, etc.) believes and trusts in Him, will not face eternal damnation, but rather, will receive the free gift of eternal life through Jesus Christ."*

By expounding on the verse, I hope you will understand God's great love for you, no matter who you are!

Gary Smalley, a well-known speaker and author, always talks about having a sense of awe about the things we value. That which we find valuable we want to endure forever, thus we love it or them. I think we have cheapened the word, by using

Cross Words – Week 2 - LOVE

it for everyday things like, "I love my car!"

In the Greek language, there are various words to define love: Phileo, Eros, and Agape. Phileo is like the common love between people in general (friendship). Eros is the intimate love, and Agape is the unconditional love.

Love is more than a feeling, it is an inner desire or way of thinking that always endures. And God's Love is a perfect, unconditional love, the type we should all strive to achieve a likeness to.

1 John 14:16-18 states;
> [16] *God is love. Whoever lives in love lives in God, and God in him.* [17] *In this way, love is made complete among us so that we will have confidence on the Day of Judgment, because in this world we are like him.*

What is love?

1 Corinthians 13:4-8;
> [4] *"Love is patient, love is kind. It does not envy, it does not boast, it is not proud.* [5] *It is not rude, it is not self-seeking, it is not easily angered, and it keeps no record of wrongs.* [6] *Love does not delight in evil but rejoices with the truth.* [7] *It always protects, always trusts, always hopes, and always perseveres.* [8] *Love never fails."*

Cross Words – Week 2 - LOVE

1 John 4:7-12;

> [7] Dear friends, let us love one another, for love comes from God. Everyone who loves has been born of God and knows God. [8] Whoever does not love does not know God, because God is love. [9] This is how God showed his love among us: He sent his one and only Son into the world that we might live through him. [10] This is love: not that we loved God, but that he loved us and sent his Son as an atoning sacrifice for our sins. [11] Dear friends, since God so loved us, we also ought to love one another. [12] No one has ever seen God; but if we love one another, God lives in us and his love is made complete in us.

What can separate us from God's love?

Romans 8:35-39;

> [35] Who shall separate us from the love of Christ? Shall trouble or hardship or persecution or famine or nakedness or danger or sword? [36] As it is written: "For your sake we face death all day long we are considered as sheep to be slaughtered." [37] No, in all these things we are more than conquerors through him who loved us. [38] For I am convinced that neither death nor life, neither angels nor demons, neither the present nor the future, nor any powers, [39] neither height nor depth, nor anything else in all creation, will be able to separate us from the love of God that is in Christ Jesus our Lord.

Absolutely nothing can separate us from God's love. We, on the other hand, can choose not to love God, yet He still loves us. He has the perfect, unconditional love. He loves us so

Cross Words – Week 2 - LOVE

much that He gave His Son to die for us, so that we may be reconciled with Him.

Deuteronomy 7:9;

> [9] *Know therefore that the LORD your God is God; he is the faithful God, keeping his covenant of love to a thousand generations of those who love him and keep his commands*

1 John 3:1;

> [1] *How great is the love the Father has lavished on us, that we should be called children of God! And that is what we are! The reason the world does not know us is that it did not know him.*

The point is---God <u>really</u> loves you! It doesn't matter who you were, only who you have become through being born again in Christ.

How should I love God?

Deuteronomy 6:5;

"Love the LORD your God with all your heart and with all your soul and with all your strength."
    Or as I heard a Pastor interpret it,
"Love the Lord your God, with all your passion, intellect, prayer, and power."

Cross Words – Week 2 - LOVE

In other words, love God with all that is within you, and all that you are capable of feeling, thinking, praying for, and able to accomplish. Give Him your all- all the time!

Just like with joy, though, too many people attempt to fulfill their love in other people. We live in sad times, when men and women are conning each other by telling them, "I love you".

Jeff Warner, founder of Ultimate Strength, said, "Women, don't listen to a man's words, rather watch his actions. Does he show you that he truly loves and cares for you, or is he just after something? If they really love you, they can wait!"

Remember, love is more than how we *feel* about someone or something; rather, it is how we value them. Love is a decision!

Recommended reading:
Love for a lifetime by Dr. James Dobson

In this book, Dr. Dobson emphasizes the benefits of staying committed to the marriage. Look at the couples that have been married for 25 or more years, there must be some cord that has held the two together other than just commitment; and that

Cross Words – Week 2 - LOVE

cord is Jesus and the love that He gives to us. I commend those of you who have stayed committed for so many years!

- ❖ Name some people/things that are valuable to you:
  - ○ --On a separate piece of paper, write down who/what is valuable to you. List the "things" on one side, and people on the other. Which do you find more valuable?

- ❖ It is those things that we value, that we want to Endure through the good times and bad. When you fall in **LOVE** with someone, discover what you value in them, always.

- ❖ God's **LOVE** is the sweetest, most perfect LOVE we could ever receive – His is unconditional! He valued us so much that He sent His own Son to die for us.

Prayer

Father, thank you for your awesome LOVE. You are the Author and Father of LOVE. Help me to value everyone in this life. Without LOVE, "I am nothing more than a noisy gong." I want to LOVE others so that they may experience peace and your grace in their life. Jesus, I love you, because you first loved me, even though I was not deserving of your LOVE. Amen.

PRAY

Power Resounds Around You

Ephesians 3: 16, 17;

> *[16] "I <u>pray</u> that out of his glorious riches He may strengthen you with power through His Spirit in your inner being, [17] so that Christ may dwell in your hearts through faith."*

Jeremiah 29: 11, 12;

> *[11] "For I know the plans I have for you", declares the LORD, "plans to prosper you and not to harm you, plans to give you hope and a future. [12] Then you will call upon Me and come and <u>pray</u> to Me, and I will listen to you."*

When you pray, there is power from God that resounds around you. You are no longer fighting the battle alone; rather, you are requesting reinforcements to aid you. In Medieval times, if a soldier was in need of reinforcements, he would sound a horn or some other alarm to request help. Other soldiers would then come to his rescue and surround him. In the Book of Judges, the Israelites, commanded by the Lord and Gideon, had fought an enemy with only a few soldiers who blew trumpets and broke jars that made a resounding noise that caused the enemy to be confused and fight each other.

Cross Words – Week 2 - PRAY

Pray for others everyday! When you can't help in other ways, be it financially or emotionally, pray. The power you can bestow on another person is tremendous, especially when you realize the One who is always listening to our prayers – God. When you disagree with someone – Pray about it! When you are worried about something – Pray about it! When you love someone – Pray for them! When you want to see your life improve – Pray to the one who can show you how...Jesus!

In the "Lord's Prayer", Jesus does not just give us another prayer; rather He teaches us *how* to pray.

Matthew 6:5-15;

> [5] *"And when you pray, do not be like the hypocrites, for they love to pray standing in the synagogues and on the street corners to be seen by men. I tell you the truth, they have received their reward in full.* [6] *But when you pray, go into your room, close the door and pray to your Father, who is unseen. Then your Father, who sees what is done in secret, will reward you.* [7] *And when you pray, do not keep on babbling like pagans, for they think they will be heard because of their many words.* [8] *Do not be like them, for your Father knows what you need before you ask him.*
>
> [9] *"This, then, is how you should pray:*
>
> *" `Our Father in heaven,*

Cross Words – Week 2 - PRAY

hallowed be your name,
[10] your kingdom come,
  your will be done
    on earth as it is in heaven.

[11] Give us today our daily bread.

[12] Forgive us our debts,
  as we also have forgiven our debtors.

[13] And lead us not into temptation,
  but deliver us from the evil one. '

[14] For if you forgive men when they sin against you, your heavenly Father will also forgive you. [15] But if you do not forgive men their sins, your Father will not forgive your sins.

❖ Find more opportunities to **PRAY** this week – for others and yourself. Be in communication with the One who listens.

❖ Real power is found when we are on our knees – in Prayer.

❖ People I can **PRAY** for this week:

Cross Words – Week 2 - PRAY

PRAYER

Father, I am thankful that you sent Jesus to break down the barrier between us and you so that we can come before you as we PRAY. I desire to talk with you more, to know you, to love you, to hear you. Please help me to spend more time in prayer with you for others and for my own life. I know that your Power Resounds Around our prayers. You are the answer to all my prayers. I love you. Amen.

Week 3

GOD

Do you really know Him?

GOD – **G**reat **O**mnipotent **D**esigner

JESUS – **J**oy **E**ternal **S**hows **U**s **S**alvation

LORD – **L**et **O**ur **R**edeemer **D**ecide

AWE – **A**mazing **W**onders **E**veryday

Cross Words – Week 3 - GOD

GOD

Great Omnipotent Designer

God is very Great, He is all-powerful (Omnipotent) and He alone designed and created the whole universe with the words of His mouth. No other god can have such a claim!

Colossians 1:16-20;

> [16] *For by him all things were created: things in heaven and on earth, visible and invisible, whether thrones or powers or rulers or authorities; all things were created by him and for him.* [17] *He is before all things, and in him all things hold together.* [18] *And he is the head of the body, the church; he is the beginning and the firstborn from among the dead, so that in everything he might have the supremacy.* [19] *For God was pleased to have all his fullness dwell in him,* [20] *and through him to reconcile to himself all things, whether things on earth or things in heaven, by making peace through his blood, shed on the cross."*

God is God, and He is coming back for us, whether we believe it or not. He is Sovereign! He is the Master of everything. He is the Great I Am. It gives us a tremendous sense of awe, knowing He created everything, yet came to earth to reconcile our relationship with Him.

Cross Words – Week 3 - GOD

Hebrews 11:6

> *⁶ And without faith it is impossible to please God, because anyone who comes to him must believe that he exists and that he rewards those who earnestly seek him.*

- ❖ God is God – this is both truth and reality.

- ❖ Do you believe and trust in God?

- ❖ Take time this week to focus on the Great things God has done, both in this world and in your own life.

- ❖ He alone is all-powerful (Omnipotent), so humbly come before Him this week and realize who He really is.

Prayer

Father God, I thank you that you are the Great Omnipotent Designer, no one else comes close to your awesome majesty and power. You are my one and only God. I am determined to put no other gods before you, such as things of this world that take my focus off of you. I vow to let go of those things and focus on You alone. Amen.

Cross Words – Week 3 - JESUS

JESUS

Joy Eternal Shows Us Salvation

YESHUA

Yahweh Enables Salvation Helping Us All

(Hebrew name for Jesus)

John 14:6

Jesus said unto him, "I am the way, the truth and the life; no man comes unto the Father but by me."

He is the only one who can give us true joy and show us that the only way to Heaven is through Him. Having joy in life does give us purpose and reason to live, yet if that joy isn't Jesus and His gift of Salvation, then we have only a temporal joy. Jesus came into this world to show us the Way of Salvation.

It gives me great joy, even during the worst of times, to know that I am saved and will spend my eternal life with Jesus. Yes we will all experience eternal life, but it is up to us whether we spend it, with great joy, in Heaven with Jesus or in Hell

Cross Words – Week 3 - JESUS

suffering forever.

Remember the decision is yours. I hope and pray that you will choose Jesus, the source of all hope and joy. He is the answer.

- ❖ JESUS is the only Way for us to receive Eternal life.
- ❖ Who is JESUS to you?
- ❖ JESUS is the true source of joy.
- ❖ Have you accepted His gift of Salvation in your life?

Prayer

Father, I thank you so much for sending JESUS into this world to save us, and to give us real joy. Jesus, reveal yourself to me this week and every day of my life. LORD Jesus, I want to ask you into my heart right here and now. I want you to be my personal Lord and Savior. I desire to tell others of your wondrous joy that you give to those you love. Amen.

Cross Words – Week 3 - LORD

<u>LORD</u>
Let Our Redeemer Decide

1 Samuel 24:15;
 [15] *May the LORD be our judge and decide between us.*

When we ask Jesus to be Lord of our life, we are actually asking Him to decide for us on the important things in life, to have the respected control of the rest of our lives. No, we are not to be like puppets; rather we are to serve Him with joy and thanksgiving.

In Medieval times, the lord of the manor was the man in charge of all the people under him. He could decide what job you were to do, based on his need. If the lord was good, he would treat his servants well and the servants found peace and purpose knowing that they were well taken care of.

Our Lord and Savior has the best plan for your life, so let Him decide. Let the Lord be the Lord of your life, and then you will have peace.

Cross Words – Week 3 - LORD

- *Is Jesus the Lord of your life?*
- What areas of your life do you need to let Him Decide on?
- He is our Redeemer that paid the price for us, so that we could be set free.
- This week, reflect on how JESUS is LORD, and how He desires to bring hope and order to your life.

Prayer

Father, I thank you again and again for Jesus. I am grateful that He is the LORD of my life. I ask, through grace, that you would help me to surrender those areas of my life that I need Him to Decide on. I know when I do, I will be happier and more at peace. LORD Jesus, I want to ask you into my heart right here and now. I love you. Amen.

Cross Words – Week 3 - AWE

AWE
Amazing Wonders Everyday

Job 25:2;

"Dominion and awe belong to God; he establishes order in the heights of heaven.

When I think about the awesome works that God has done, both in the created world and in the miracles I have seen, I am amazed that God cares about us so much everyday.

I like the song, "I stand in awe of you", it reminds me that God is Sovereign and still in control. Though He is my Personal Lord and Savior, I must also remember that He is God. My poem below shows of how AWEsome He is and why He did it.

Awestruck

In awe I stand before you
As I reflect on what you have done
I am amazed at your creation
But mostly of your Son.

Cross Words – Week 3 - AWE

I know I am not worthy,
And I wonder how someone so small
Could ever please such an awesome God
Or offer you anything at all.

I'll give you my heart,
Though it is broken and lost,
For I know the most precious wonder,
Is that you saved us at a great cost.

❖ What makes you stand in AWE of God?

❖ Everyday, think of a new and AWEsome way to recognize the beauty and wonder of God.

Prayer

Father, I am in AWE of all the Amazing Wonders that you show me Everyday. Help me to see and appreciate them. They are so wonderful, and can brighten even the darkest of days. Father, you are AWEsome! Amen

Week 4

CROSS

Do you want to be rescued?

CROSS – **C**hrist **R**escued **O**ur **S**inful **S**ouls

SAVED – **S**ecure **A**nd **V**ictorious **E**dge **D**aily

PEACE – **P**ut **E**verything **A**t **C**hrist's **E**nthronement

ROCK – **R**est **O**n **C**hrist's **K**ingship

Cross Words – Week 4 - CROSS

CROSS

Christ Rescued Our Sinful Souls

1 Timothy 1:15;

"Here is a trustworthy saying that deserves full acceptance: <u>Christ</u> Jesus came into the world to <u>rescue</u> sinners..."

Galatians 1:3-5;

³ Grace and peace to you from God our Father and the Lord Jesus Christ, ⁴ who gave himself for our sins to <u>rescue us</u> from the present evil age, according to the will of our God and Father, ⁵ to whom be glory for ever and ever. Amen

1 Corinthians 9:15;

¹⁵ Thanks be to God for his indescribable gift!

Cross Words – Week 4 - CROSS

Christ Rescued Our Sinful Souls, thus, we owe Him only one thing, our life! There are really two parts to this phrase:

> 1: I must acknowledge that Christ is the One who rescued our souls.
>
> And--
>
> 2: That we were sinners, and yet He rescued us.

With that in mind, those are like the steps to become a Christian. Take for instance the scripture:

Romans 10:9,10;

> [9] *That if you confess with your mouth, "Jesus is Lord," and believe in your heart that God raised Him from the dead, you will be saved.* [10] *For it is with your heart that you believe and are justified, and it is with your mouth that you confess and are saved.*

If you haven't already done so, I urge you to allow the Lord to "Rescue" you, to allow Him to be Lord over your life.

John 18:36;

> *"So, if the Son has set you free, you will be free indeed."*

Cross Words – Week 4 - CROSS

Again, we must realize that, yes, Christ rescued us, and because He rescued us, we would desire not to sin again. I am not saying that we will never sin once we have given our heart over to Jesus, however I am saying that we must strive to avoid being sinful to show our gratitude to the One who Saved us.

Jesus said to the adulterous woman in **Matthew 8:11;**
> *"Then neither do I condemn you," Jesus declared. "Go now and <u>leave</u> your life of sin."*

When you see someone wearing a cross necklace, take the time to ask them if they know what it means. I did that with a man and his girlfriend entering the hotel to check-in the same time I was. He mentions the usual, "Ah, it's one of those Christian things." So, I said, "Do you mind if I share another definition of it?" and that is when I shared with him the **CROSS** acronym. I think it hit something in him, because he looked like he had seen a ghost and then he told his girlfriend that he couldn't have this type of relationship anymore and they left the hotel and I didn't see them there again. Don't forget the "sinner's prayer" is all in this one word.

If someone purchased a "Purple Heart" medal at an estate sale,

Cross Words – Week 4 - CROSS

and then put it on their shirt to wear everywhere they went, don't you think the military men and women who earned one would feel a little bit bothered by this? Wearing a **CROSS** should be a statement of our Faith in Jesus. Though I am glad that people wear the **CROSS** because it looks "Cool", I pray they learn the real meaning of it. However, wearing a cross doesn't make you a Christian anymore than wearing a set of "Wings" makes you a pilot.

God provides the key to get into peoples hearts; you must discover what that key is in each person you are witnessing to. I hope that these acronyms serve as tools to discover these keys. Have you ever tried to turn a light-switch on by just feeling around the walls of a room? The lights will not go on until you have flipped the switch that enables the lights to go on, and this only after you have gained access to the room. Take time to get to know people, in order to get into their heart's door, and then help them find their way in life by showing them the switch to "enlighten" their lives.

Cross Words – Week 4 - CROSS

- ❖ Have you allowed Christ to Rescue you?

- ❖ If you wear a **CROSS**, wear it with honor, especially now that you know its meaning.

- ❖ Take time to thank the Lord for paying for your sins on the **CROSS**.

PRAYER

Father, thank you for sending your Son, Jesus, to suffer and die on the CROSS as an atonement for our sins. Help me to appreciate your gift by living a life that is holy and acceptable to you. Jesus, thank you for rescuing me and bridging the gap between us and the Father. You died for me so now I'll live for you. Amen

Cross Words – Week 4 - SAVED

<u>SAVED</u>

Secure And Victorious Edge Daily

Hebrews 10:39;

[39] But we are not of those who shrink back and are destroyed, but of those who believe and are <u>saved</u>.

Did you know that you could actually know you are saved (going to heaven)? Now that you have taken the first step of faith, and now desire to follow Christ intimately everyday, you can have an assurance that your place in Heaven is waiting for you. Consider these Scriptures that speak of this assurance:

Romans 10:9,13;

[9] That if you confess with your mouth, "Jesus is Lord," and believe in your heart that God raised him from the dead, you will be saved. ,.... [13] for, "Everyone who calls on the name of the Lord will be saved."

Ephesians 4: 30;

[30] "And do not grieve the Holy Spirit of God, with whom you were sealed for the day of redemption.

Cross Words – Week 4 – SAVED

Romans 6: 3-11;

> [3] Or don't you know that all of us who were baptized into Christ Jesus were baptized into his death? [4] We were therefore buried with him through baptism into death in order that, just as Christ was raised from the dead through the glory of the Father, we too may live a new life. [5] If we have been united with him like this in his death, we will certainly also be united with him in his resurrection. [6] For we know that our old self was crucified with him so that the body of sin might be done away with, that we should no longer be slaves to sin-- [7] because anyone who has died has been freed from sin. [8] Now if we died with Christ, we believe that we will also live with him. [9] For we know that since Christ was raised from the dead, he cannot die again; death no longer has mastery over him. [10] The death he died, he died to sin once for all; but the life he lives, he lives to God. [11] In the same way, count yourselves dead to sin but alive to God in Christ Jesus.

1 Peter 1: 3-9;

> [3] Praise be to the God and Father of our Lord Jesus Christ! In his great mercy he has given us new birth into a living hope through the resurrection of Jesus Christ from the dead, [4] and into an inheritance that can never perish, spoil or fade--kept in heaven for you, [5] who through faith are shielded by God's power until the coming of the salvation that is ready to be revealed in the last time. [6] In this you greatly rejoice, though now for a little while you may have had to suffer grief in all kinds of trials. [7] These have come so that your faith--of greater worth than gold, which perishes even though refined by

Cross Words – Week 4 – SAVED

> *fire--may be proved genuine and may result in praise, glory and honor when Jesus Christ is revealed. [8] Though you have not seen him, you love him; and even though you do not see him now, you believe in him and are filled with an inexpressible and glorious joy, [9] for you are receiving the goal of your faith, the salvation of your souls.*

Titus 3: 4-7;

> [4] *But when the kindness and love of God our Savior appeared, [5] he saved us, not because of righteous things we had done, but because of his mercy. He saved us through the washing of rebirth and renewal by the Holy Spirit, [6] whom he poured out on us generously through Jesus Christ our Savior, [7] so that, having been justified by his grace, we might become heirs having the hope of eternal life."*

1 John 5:13

> *These things I have written to you who believe in the name of the Son of God, <u>that you may know that you have eternal life</u> and that you may continue to believe in the name of the Son of God.*

Pastor J. Michael Morris, a former pastor of mine, asked me, "Nick, what does it mean to have a victory?"

I said, "Well, isn't it when you win a battle?"

"Yes." He exclaimed. "And it seems like you have a lot of battles to fight, and the more battles you fight the better the chances to win. So stay in the fight, learn from them, and you will be Victorious."

Cross Words – Week 4 – SAVED

- ❖ Are you Saved?
- ❖ Do you want a Victorious Edge in your life?
- ❖ This week, take time to reflect on the day you were Saved by Jesus. Also, pray for unsaved loved ones, that they too might have eternal life.

Prayer

Father, thank you for saving me through your Son, Jesus. I have been drowning in this sea of life, and there you were to reach out and rescue me. I know that I am SAVED now. Wow! What an awesome thought! I know that I will spend eternity with you. Because you SAVED me, help me to live every day here showing others of how they too can be rescued. I love you. Amen.

Cross Words – Week 4 – PEACE

PEACE

Put **E**verything **A**t **C**hrist's **E**nthronement

Philippians 4:7

> *⁷ And the peace of God, which transcends all understanding, will guard your hearts and your minds in Christ Jesus.*

Christ died, rose from the dead, and then ascended into Heaven, and is enthroned at the right-hand of God having authority over sin and death. The Father exalted Him to the Highest place, because He was willing to humble Himself and die for our sins. Many call Christ's throne "The Mercy Seat", and since He is full of love and compassion and has bore all our burdens already, won't you allow Him to handle your problems today by putting them at His feet?

Jesus said in **John 14:27;**

> *"Peace I leave with you; my peace I give you. I do not give to you as the world gives. Do not let your hearts be troubled and do not be afraid."*

Sometimes I tease my kids in the car by saying, "Let's go for a ride to someplace fun!" With excited anticipation they respond

Cross Words – Week 4 – PEACE

with, "Where?" To which I say, "You'll find out when we get there." It almost always turns into a fun time. God wants us to realize that He is in the driver seat and He knows the Way. Just wait on Him, and find PEACE in Him.

He is the Peace that passes all understanding and He will never pass away.

To have a piece of Peace, you must have the Peace of God.

Or one I had seen on a bumper sticker:
"No God, No Peace -
Know God, Know Peace."

The Apostles were certainly not at peace, there on the open sea faced with horrendous storm. Looking to Jesus, they see that He is resting! No, it's not because Jesus doesn't care that He could rest, rather it is because He was so at peace with the Father. He was then able to say to the wind and waves, "Peace, be still!", and He is able to do this with the storms in our life. Be careful though, the disciples asked Jesus to end the storm, leaving them with a new dilemma …stuck in the middle of the sea with no wind to carry their sailboat to shore. Don't

Cross Words – Week 4 – PEACE

ask Him to end the storm, rather to carry you safely through it.

- ❖ PEACE can only come through God.

- ❖ The throne of Christ is only place to release our problems.

- ❖ This week, think about the people and situations that you can put at the throne of Christ.

Prayer

Heavenly Father, I thank you so much for sending your Only Son, Jesus, to come to Earth to share in our heartaches and pains, and to rescue us by bearing all the sin of the world on His own shoulders by taking up the cross, willingly, and dying for each one that will call on His Name. Jesus, I am amazed by the awesome power the Heavenly Father has bestowed upon you, like calming the sea for the disciples; I pray, Lord God, that you will calm the storms in the lives of your people. Help me to grow because of the storms in my life and the lives of your people. Help me to realize that you are the Master of everything. Thank you Jesus for what you have done for me. "You are our Peace that has broken down every wall." I know that when I place my problems at your feet, trusting in your unfailing love and power, I too will have peace. I love you! Amen!

Cross Words – Week 4 – ROCK

ROCK
Rest On Christ's Kingship

1 Corinthians 10:3,4;

> [3] *They all ate the same spiritual food* [4] *and drank the same spiritual drink; for they drank from the spiritual rock that accompanied them, <u>and that rock was Christ.</u>*

Matthew 7:24-27;

> [24] *"Therefore everyone who hears these words of mine and puts them into practice is like a wise man who built his house on the rock.* [25] *The rain came down, the streams rose, and the winds blew and beat against that house; yet it did not fall, because it had its foundation on the rock.* [26] *But everyone who hears these words of mine and does not put them into practice is like a foolish man who built his house on sand.* [27] *The rain came down, the streams rose, and the winds blew and beat against that house, and it fell with a great crash."*

Where is **_your faith_** at this time in your life? Is it built on the solid rock, or are you relying on your own strength and understanding - on a foundation of sand. Are there areas of your faith that need strengthening? Are you willing to leave your house on sand, just to start over on a house built on a solid rock?

Cross Words – Week 4 – ROCK

Anyone that has ever been caught in a flood knows one thing; the rushing water is not a safe place to be. It would be safer to find a solid rock that is on higher ground. If the water becomes higher, you could rest assured that the rock won't move and that the water probably won't rise up over it. The reason it won't move is because its base is deep within the ground.

Jesus is that solid rock that cannot be shaken. He is the King of kings and the Lord of Lords. He is the one who can give you rest through the pain.

2 Samuel 22:2-4;

> 2 "The Lord is my <u>rock</u>, my fortress and my deliverer;
>
> 3 my God is my <u>rock</u>, in whom I take refuge,
> my shield and the horn of my salvation.
> He is my stronghold, my refuge and my savior--
> from violent men you save me.
> 4 I call to the Lord, who is worthy of praise,
> and I am saved from my enemies.

- ❖ Jesus Christ is the King of kings and Lord of lords.
- ❖ Are you ready to find peace and rest in Him?
- ❖ This week, find more ways to Rest On Christ's Kingship.

Cross Words – Week 4 – ROCK

PRAYER

Father, I thank you that gave Jesus as the King and Lord of my life. I ask you to help me to Rest in Him, knowing that He has the power and compassion to handling any problems that come my way. When the floods of life come my way, show me that I can find solace and safety in Him. He was, is, and always will be... the Rock of ages. Amen

Week 5

GROW

What does it take to GROW in the Lord?

GROW – **G**ain **R**eal **O**ngoing **W**isdom

PURE – **P**erfect **U**ntainted **R**esolve **E**veryday

CHOICE – **C**onsider **H**ow **O**ur **I**nput **C**hanges **E**verything

HEAR – **H**eed **E**verything **A**nd **R**espond

Cross Words – Week 4 – GROW

GROW
Gain Real Ongoing Wisdom

2 Corinthians 10:15;
Our hope is that, as your faith continues to grow,....

It takes Wisdom to know when to take the next step of faith, and to understand the meaning of each step. It helps if this is Real, Godly Wisdom, and not that of the world. This Wisdom must be working in our lives on a continual (Ongoing) basis. Moreover, to attain (Gain) this kind of Wisdom is greater than having all the riches in the world.

There are many Scriptures that speak specifically of gaining Wisdom. Here are five to keep in mind.

Proverbs 8:11,12;
[11] for wisdom more precious than rubies, and nothing you desire can compare with her. [12] "I, wisdom, dwell together with prudence; I possess knowledge and discretion."

Cross Words – Week 5 - GROW

Psalm 90:12;

> *Teach us to number our days aright,
> that we may gain a heart of wisdom.*

Proverbs 21:11;

> *When a mocker is punished, the simple gain wisdom; when a wise man is instructed, he gets knowledge.*

Acts 7:10;

> *"He gave Joseph wisdom and enabled him to gain the goodwill of Pharaoh king of Egypt; so he made him ruler over Egypt and all his palace."*

And, James 1:5;

> *[5] If any of you lacks wisdom, he should ask God, who gives generously to all without finding fault, and it will be given to him.*

So, if you want to attain perfect Faith, you must ask for Wisdom, right from the beginning. God gives Wisdom to all who ask.

Though we strive for perfect wisdom, it will not be perfect until we are actually before the face of God. That is when all that we have trusted and believed in will be made fully known to us.

❖ What does it take to make a flower grow?
- o it needs to start with a seed
- o it needs good soil
- o it needs water and sunlight
- o it needs time

❖ This similar to our spiritual growth….
- o we need to be as a seed (Saved)
- o and be planted in good soil (place of worship where we can grow),
- o have water and sunlight (instructions and fellowship, and the Light of Son),
- o and finally, time (wait on the Lord to use you and then GROW in Him).

❖ Do you lack Wisdom? Ask God to give it to you today.

❖ Remember, it must be Ongoing in order to grow.

PRAYER

Father, thank you so much that you are willing to offer Wisdom to anyone who will ask for it. Help me to grow in Wisdom every day. When I lack Wisdom, speak to me through your precious Holy Spirit. Amen.

Cross Words – Week 5 - PURE

PURE
Perfect **U**ntainted **R**esolve **E**veryday

Psalm 19: 9,10;

> [9] *"The fear of the LORD is **pure**, enduring forever. The ordinances of the LORD are sure and altogether righteous.* [10] *They are more precious than gold, than much **pure** gold; they are sweeter than honey, than honey from the comb.*

Again, I urge you to live a life that is PURE and HOLY. Many would rather buy something when they know it is pure. Take honey, for example; why do you think they put on the label "Pure Honey"? Because it makes the honey that much more valuable, since it is straight from the hive. The honey is then considered perfect, because unnecessary additives have not tainted it.

Being pure means to be untainted by the world and all it wants to offer us. I have asked many people if they have ever really attained all that it has to offer. Usually I get, "Not really." That is when I like to ask them, "Do you know how people can get a stubborn donkey to move?"

Cross Words – Week 5 - PURE

They respond with, "No."

So I say, "They tie a stick to the donkey's collar and then hang an apple down from the stick, just out of reach of the donkey. The donkey will mindlessly chase after the apple, yet it never gets it.

That is how the world is with us... it offers us great things that never really satisfy us. All I want to do is give you the apple so you will be satisfied, and then do things because you received it, not because you had to chase for it."

People don't talk much of staying PURE before marriage anymore. It is essential to having a successful marriage. Abstaining from sex before marriage will help prevent STDs and will cause you to value the person and their personality, the way God intended it to be.

- ❖ Scripture says:
- ❖ *"How does a man keep his way <u>PURE</u>, be living according to your Word."* **Psalm 119: 9**
- ❖ Would you say you have kept your life PURE?
- ❖ If not, do you realize that you can still develop a resolve today to have a life that is PURE?

Cross Words – Week 5 - PURE

- ❖ This week, focus on perfecting your resolve to be pure.
  - o What might detour you from this resolve?
  - o What benefits might you receive from keeping your resolve?

PRAYER

Father, I desire to live a life that is pure and holy. Though the enemy should attempt to distract me, I pray that you help to have the resolve to stay strong and pure. Though I am not perfect, You are, and with you I can do all things. I commit today to keep my eyes focused on you. I love you for who you are. Amen.

Cross Words – Week 5 - CHOICE

CHOICE

Consider **H**ow **O**ur **I**nput **C**hanges **E**verything

Acts 15:7-9;

> *"Brothers, you know that some time ago <u>God made a choice</u> among you that the Gentiles might hear from my lips the message of the gospel and believe. 8 God, who knows the heart, showed that he accepted them by giving the Holy Spirit to them, just as he did to us. 9 He made no distinction between us and them, for he purified their hearts by faith.*

We have a **CHOICE** in life, to live right and have eternal life, or to choose the wrong path and face eternal damnation. It's our choice! We have such a loving Father that He does not force us to follow Him! A child that is given a choice usually lives a much healthier life. For example, if I give one of my children the choice of eating what's on their plate or no dessert, they will usually ponder it for a moment then decide that it's better to eat what they have and not miss out on the wonderful dessert.

It is up to you to consider how your input (decision) can truly change everything in your life, whether it is spiritual or non-

Cross Words – Week 5 - CHOICE

spiritual.

If you make right choices in life, you will have nothing to fear, Wrong choices tend to haunt us later. As with the acronym, our decisions (or input) can change everything in our life! Wrong choices I made as a child still affect me today. If I could change anything in life, I would've made much better choices; it would have saved me a lot of pain and heartache.

Joshua 24:15;

> *"But if serving the **LORD** seems undesirable to you, then choose for yourselves this day whom you will serve, whether the gods your forefathers served beyond the River, or the gods of the Amorites, in whose land you are living. But as for me and my household, we will serve the **LORD**."*

- ❖ What CHOICEs have you made that you can be proud of? Are there ones that you wish you hadn't Considered doing?

- ❖ Are you willing to make a CHOICE today to Change the rest of your life by following Jesus?

- ❖ It is your CHOICE – so make it a good one.

PRAYER

Father, I thank you that you have given me the free CHOICE to follow you. What a loving God you are! Help me to make the right Input (Decision) in the things I do today. Amen.

Cross Words – Week 5 - HEAR

HEAR
Heed Everything And Respond

Revelation 13:9;

"He who has an ear, let him hear."

Many times people would ask me, "Did you even hear what I said?" and I have to admit, there are times when I did not hear them because I was not paying attention to what they were saying. When you hear something, to be really listening, you must take in all that you have heard and then respond to it. There is a saying "Kill two birds with one stone"; I like to see if people are really listening by saying, "Kill two stones with one bird".

There are those who have ears to hear but don't listen. There are those with eyes to see and yet have no vision. If we would just stop and listen, our vision would be made clearer.

In his book, *12 Seeds of Successful Relationships*, Norm Andersen states *"Listening goes beyond simply hearing*

Cross Words – Week 5 - HEAR

something. Listening involves actually heeding – that is, noticing and considering something – so that it affects a person's thoughts or behavior. Physically hearing a train whistle is only part of listening. Heeding the warning – stopping to let the train pass – is a fuller form of listening that yields a life-saving result…

When listening grows, people receive the attention they need. They are able to express themselves, and voice their fears, needs, joys and dreams. People show they care about others when they listen, and are willing to invest time to be with them. The gift of listening is a gift that another person may treasure for a lifetime."

- ❖ What might prevent you from actually hearing someone?
- ❖ Why do you think people don't respond to what was said?
- ❖ Listening is a very important tool for having a better relationship – with God and others.

Cross Words – Week 5 - HEAR

PRAYER

Father, I pray that I will learn to hear what you are speaking to me. I choose to respond to your leading, according to your Word and Will. "Speak Lord, for your servant is listening". (1 Samuel 3:9) Help me to take more time to listen to others…to really hear what they are saying. Amen.

Week 6

<u>FEAR</u>

What prevents you from knowing God?

FEAR – **F**inding **E**verything **A** **R**oadblock

DOUBT – **D**epending **O**n **U**nderstanding **B**efore **T**rusting

GUILT – **G**etting **U**s **I**nto **L**iving **T**errified

SHAME – **S**uffering **H**as **A** **M**easured **E**ffect

Cross Words – Week 6 - FEAR

FEAR

Finding Everything A Roadblock

Isaiah 43:1;

> "*Fear not, for I have redeemed you; I have summoned you by name; you are mine.*"

Isaiah 54:14;

> "*You shall establish yourself in righteousness (rightness, in conformity with God's will and order): you shall be far from even the thought of oppression or destruction, for you shall not fear, and from terror, for it shall not come near you.*"

I heard fear described like this: "Fear is the darkroom where negatives are developed." Fear is a perverted faith. It develops out of a concern of personal loss or the idea that God really won't be true to His Word. We have to realize that God is not like men; He cannot lie and He will never forsake or leave us no matter what circumstances are or what we "feel" they are. We are to be a people, a peculiar people, who walk by faith and not by sight.

Cross Words – Week 6 - FEAR

Keep in mind, there are two types of roadblocks – ones that are there by chance (tires, trees, garbage, etc.), and those that are put there on purpose (barricade to block passage).

The ones that are by chance are ones that can be removed so that we can get on our way again. These are like the fears we have in this life… fear of the dark, spiders, etc. I will cover the other type in a moment.

I went with my son on an incredible field trip for his 5th grade class, to Wolf Ridge Environmental Learning Center in Finland, MN. They teach the kids about the environment, not only their physical environment (rivers, trees, ecosystems, etc.) but also their psychological environment. There were two challenges that the students had to encounter a "Rock wall" and a "Rope bridge".

When we came to the Adventure ropes, there was a small tree blocking the path to the stairway leading to the event. I asked a few of the boys in the class to assist me with moving the tree out of our way, enabling us to accomplish what we had come there to do.

Cross Words – Week 6 - FEAR

Many of the students struggled with one challenge or the other due to their fear of falling, even though they were tethered to the course with harnesses and had a lot of support from those below. Some quickly faced their fear and conquered it; others though, found the fear to be too great to continue. Thus, they were not able to go on and enjoy the feeling of finishing the whole course. I began to realize that the worse that could happen to me there would be to fall and face my death, but what have I to fear when I know that I will be immediately escorted into Heaven! *When you don't fear death, it is much easier to live life.*

There were, on the site, many beautiful paths to walk on, and occasionally there would be a tree blocking the path, I lifted up the tree out of the way, allowing us to continue on our way. Remove the obstacles and get on your way!

What of the Fear of God? Is that also like a roadblock? Yes! The Fear of God is a roadblock that is meant to stay there, or you may find serious consequences.

Psalm 110:11

"The Fear of God is the beginning of wisdom"

Cross Words – Week 6 - FEAR

Picture in your mind a deep canyon with a bridge to cross over, but the bridge has been broken. The road construction people put up a large roadblock, with reflectors, to let you know that the bridge is out. If you choose to remove this roadblock, you'll find yourself crashing to the bottom of the canyon. God, as our loving Father, wants to protect us from the dangers in this life; we need to pay attention, have the utmost respect for his authority, and heed his warning!

- ❖ Take time this week to identify your fears.
- ❖ God can and will help you overcome your fears.
- ❖ As you slowly remove them, you will be able get back on the path God has prepared for you.
- ❖ When we FEAR God, we are actually saving ourselves from further hardship.

PRAYER

Father, I know that fear cannot abound where you are. Please help me to recognize the "roadblocks" in my life that hinder my relationship with you. I realize that these fears seem real, yet they only have the power that I give them. I am thankful that when I fear you with reverence and awe, I will be kept safe and secure. You have said, "Fear not, for I am God." My life is in your hands. Amen.

Cross Words – Week 6 - DOUBT

DOUBT

Depending **O**n **U**nderstanding **B**efore **T**rusting

Mark 11:23-24;

> *"I tell you the truth, if anyone says to this mountain, `Go, throw yourself into the sea,' and does not <u>doubt</u> in his heart but believes that what he says will happen, it will be done for him. [24] Therefore I tell you, whatever you ask for in prayer, believe that you have received it, and it will be yours."*

Proverbs 3:5;

> *Trust in the LORD with all your heart
> and <u>lean not on your own understanding</u>...*

Doubt is such a stumbling block to our faith. It causes us to lose heart, or just to depend on what *we* understand before we are willing to put our faith and trust in God or others.

James 1:6-8;

> *[6] But when he asks, he must believe and not <u>doubt</u>, because he who doubts is like a wave of the sea, blown and tossed by the wind. [7] That man should not think he will receive anything from the Lord; [8] he is a double-minded man, unstable in all he does.*

Cross Words – Week 6 - DOUBT

- ❖ To trust is challenging, however if we insist on **D**epending on **O**ur own **U**nderstanding first, we will never commit to **T**rust.

- ❖ What could you do to strengthen your trust?

- ❖ Are you willing to give up on your own understanding – which is killing both your **FAITH** and **HOPE**?

- ❖ This week, focus on the things that give you your reasons to **DOUBT**.

PRAYER

Father, I thank you that I can fully trust in you. Help me to depend on you and not my own understanding. I want to be as you would want me to be, and not lose heart because of needless DOUBT. It is not easy sometimes to let it go, but I know you can help me. I believe in you. Amen

Cross Words – Week 6 - GUILT

GUILT
Getting Us Into Living Terrified

Psalm 38:4;

"My guilt has overwhelmed me like a burden too heavy to bear."

When we do something wrong, generally we are terrified of being "found out." Guilt tends to keep us from living a fulfilled life. It causes us to spend our lives running from the things that we have done, rather than facing them. The past tends to haunt us, leaving us terrified all over again. The past tends to attempt to take over our everyday life, thus controlling us.

There is hope! God sent His Son, Jesus, to pay the price for us – through his death on the cross, to bear our sin and guilt. He became sin and guilt for us. The control that **GUILT** had on us has been broken. We can now live in peace.

Isaiah 6: 5-8;

> [5] *"Woe to me!" I cried. "I am ruined! For I am a man of unclean lips, and I live among a people of unclean lips, and my eyes have seen the King, The LORD Almighty."* [6]

Cross Words – Week 6 - GUILT

> *Then one of the seraphs flew to me with a live coal in his hand, which he had taken with tongs from the altar. [7] With it he touched my mouth and said. "See, this has touched your lips; **your guilt is taken away and your sin is atoned for**." [8] Then I heard the voice of the Lord saying, "Whom shall I send? And who will go for us?" And I said, "Here am I. Send me!"*

I imagine Isaiah was terrified of the hot coals! However, Isaiah admitted that he had unclean lips and desired to be pure. The next time you think about saying something unclean, unnecessary, and not glorifying God, think about having the hot coals touching your lips!

Consider **James 3: 7-12;**

> [7] *"All kinds of animals, reptiles, birds and creatures are being tamed and have been tamed by man, [8] but no man can tame the tongue. It is a restless evil, full of deadly poison. [9] With the tongue we praise our Lord and Father, and with it we curse men, who have been made in God's likeness. [10] Out of the same mouth come praise and cursing. My brothers, this should not be. [11] Can both fresh and salt water flow from the same spring? [12] My brothers, can a fig tree bear olives, or a grapevine bear figs? Neither can a salt spring produce fresh water."*

What helped me to deal with my filthy mouth and mind years ago was when someone shared with me from:

Cross Words – Week 6 - GUILT

Philippians 4: 8,9;

> [8] *"whatever is true, whatever is noble, whatever is right, whatever is pure, whatever is lovely, whatever is admirable – if anything is excellent or praiseworthy – think about such things.* [9] *Whatever you have learned or received or heard from me, or seen in me – put it into practice. And the God of peace will be with you."*

Colossians 3:17;

> [17] *And whatever you do, whether in word or deed, do it all in the name of the Lord Jesus, giving thanks to God the Father through him.*

Maybe you think, "I'm not going to admit my guilt, I have too much pride!" That may be the very reason you are struggling with your burden.

- ❖ Does your **GUILT** cause you to feel terrified of the consequences?

- ❖ Are you ready to give up your **GUILT** to God?

- ❖ This week, live no more in fear and terror, rather in the peace and love of Christ.

Cross Words – Week 6 - GUILT

PRAYER

Father, I thank you that you sent Jesus to this world to take my GUILT and shame upon His shoulders so that I would not have to be terrified anymore. Please forgive me of the things that I have done that offend you. I know that I must repent and change my ways. Help me live my life for you. Amen.

Cross Words – Week 6 – SHAME

SHAME
Suffering Has A Measured Effect

Isaiah 54:4;

> ⁴ *"Do not be afraid; you will not suffer <u>shame</u>. Do not fear disgrace; you will not be humiliated. You will forget the <u>shame</u> of your youth and Remember no more the reproach of your widowhood.*

Did you ever have someone tell you, "Shame on you!"? Didn't it make you feel miserable and cause you to want to change your ways? Most of the time, it leaves us feeling so miserable that we want to change the behavior. The effect it can have on our life can be measured by a changed life. Christ bore all the **SHAME** and guilt of the world upon His shoulders, so that we don't have to carry it anymore.

Romans 10:11;

> *"Anyone who trusts in him will never be put to <u>shame</u>."*

Hebrews 12:2,3;

> ² *Let us fix our eyes on Jesus, the author and perfecter of our faith, who for the joy set before him endured the cross, <u>scorning its shame</u>, and sat down at the right hand*

Cross Words – Week 6 – SHAME

of the throne of God. [3] Consider him who endured such opposition from sinful men, so that you will not grow weary and lose heart.

Proverbs 25:9,10;

*[9] If you argue your case with a neighbor,
do not betray another man's confidence,*

*[10] or he who hears it may shame you
and you will never lose your bad reputation.*

❖ What **SHAME** have you had to endure?

❖ Have you been able to measure the shame – based on your changed life?

❖ Have you given your **SHAME** and **GUILT** to Jesus?

❖ This week, focus on how someone may have shamed you and/or how you may have said this to others. What do you/they hope to gain?

Cross Words – Week 6 – SHAME

PRAYER

Father, I thank you that I no longer must pay the price for the guilt and shame in my life – Thanks to Jesus' wondrous gift of Salvation that He willingly paid for upon the Cross. I pray that the suffering I face in this world would be measured by my faith in you. Amen.

Week 7

<u>SIN</u>

Has sin mastered you?

SIN – **S**elfish **I**mperfect **N**otions

STOP – **S**in **T**raps **O**ur **P**rayer

EVIL – **E**nemy's **V**ain **I**ntentions **L**urk

LUST – **L**iving **U**nder **S**atan's **T**rap

Cross Words – Week 7 - SIN

SIN

Selfish Imperfect Notion

1 John 2:1,2;

> [1] *"My dear children, I write this to you so that you will not sin. But if anybody does sin, we have one who speaks to the Father in our defense--Jesus Christ, the Righteous One.* [2] *He is the atoning sacrifice for our sins, and not only for ours but also for the sins of the whole world.*

What would you say is your Selfish Imperfect Notions in life? Is it your temper, your critical attitude, or gossiping? Maybe it is more serious like drunkenness, sexual immorality, or causing serious harm to others.

Consider again the acronym SIN, sin is really just notions or ideas of ours that are selfish and imperfect, no matter how great or small -sin is sin. Though the notions or thoughts are not in themselves a sin, it is the action that we do because of that notion that is sin. Whether it is murdering someone, which most would agree is sin, or gossiping and lying, none of those who do so will ever enter the Kingdom of God without

Cross Words – Week 7 - SIN

repentance.

After some research, I found where we get the word "sincere" from. Many years ago, potters would make their bowls, pots, cups, and other wares. Occasionally, after finishing their wares with a shiny glaze, they would notice a crack in it. In order to sell it they would have to have something that would cover over the crack until it was purchased. Wax was used to cover the crack just enough to seal it up. Now the one who would purchase it didn't notice it until they brought it home in the hot sun, where the wax began to melt and they would then notice the crack. Annoyed, they would return to the shop and ask the potter, "Is this piece sin cere --- which translates to without (sin) wax (cere)?"

Is your life sincere? Can people detect the true flaws which you are merely trying to cover up to look good? God knows our every weakness, give it all to Him.

- ❖ Where God is, no SIN may abide.

- ❖ Submit yourself and your sins to God, and He will give you a new life.

- ❖ Are there SINs that continue to master you? Focus on those particular areas to conquer them. God will enable

Cross Words – Week 7 - SIN

❖ Because of God's Grace, we can be free of the bondage of sin – if we acknowledge it and trust in Jesus' gift of salvation to redeem us from the power of sin and death.

PRAYER

Father, you have all authority over sin and death. I am thankful for Jesus taking my place by paying the ultimate price for my sins – death on the cross. He bore the weight of all the sins of the whole world. I pray that you will help me show my eternal appreciation to Him by avoiding any sin in my life. I sincerely wish to serve you faithfully. Amen.

Cross Words – Week 7 - STOP

STOP

Sin Traps Our Prayers

1 Peter 3:7;

"Husbands, in the same way be considerate as you live with your wives, and treat them with respect as heirs with you of the gracious gift of life, so that nothing will hinder your prayers."

Isaiah 1:15;

"When you spread out your hands in prayer, I will hide my eyes from you; even if you offer many prayers, I will not listen. Your hands are full of blood";

I had heard a story about a teenage girl that wanted to go see an "R" rated movie with her friends, which her parents said no. She argued that it only had a little swearing and one brief nude scene, no big deal to her. So, her parents said they would talk it over and make a final decision in the morning. The next day, her dad made brownies, gathered the girl and her friends together and said, "If you can eat these brownies, then you can go to the show." The girls thought they had this one in the bag. Then the dad said, "By the way, the cat got sick and a

Cross Words – Week 7 - STOP

little bit accidentally got into the bowl, but it is mixed in with all that good stuff so you probably won't notice it." The girls got the message, and did not go to the movie.

Again, sin is sin, no matter how great or small. Don't let the enemy have the slightest hold on you. Remember that Christ Rescued you so you do not have to wallow in the mud of sin any longer.

- ❖ What sin in your life may be STOPping you from enjoying a great relationship with God?
- ❖ This week, ask God to forgive you of your sins.

<u>PRAYER</u>
Father, I desire to have my prayers answered by you, yet I understand that you cannot have sin come between us and you. I don't want anything to stop the wonderful relationship that you and I can have. Help me to see the areas of my life that may hinder my prayers. I ask you now to forgive me of the sin in my life so that we might have direct communication with each other. I want to live faithfully for you. Amen.

Cross Words – Week 7 - EVIL

EVIL
Enemy's Vain Intentions Lurk

From the "Lord's Prayer" **Matthew 6:13;**
"*And lead us not into temptation, but <u>deliver us from the evil one.</u>*"

I know of various women who had a child when they were 17 or younger. Now their daughters, who are now about that same age, figure, "Mom, since you had me when you were my age, what's wrong with me doing that now?" Many mothers have said, "Because I really don't want you going down that same path I went through."

Consider the following analogy:
A close friend and I went for a walk on a path deep in the woods. The woodland area around us was spectacular. We were enjoying our time together; everything seemed to be going just perfect, until a large black bear came along and began to attack us. After a narrow escape and a brief recovery period, we decide that a little attack wasn't going to stop us

Cross Words – Week 7 - EVIL

from doing what we wanted to do, so we continue down the path.

Things were going great again, until a mountain lion attacked us and nearly killed us. But, again we decided that the waterfall at the end of the path was just too phenomenal to pass up, so we continued on our walk. Little did we know that the leaves and branches on the path ahead were covering a huge pit! After stepping on the brush pile, we fell 15 feet into a very treacherous pit.

Though battered and bruised, we struggled to get out of the pit, and after many hours and a lot of blood, sweat and tears, we managed to get out. We decided it is probably best to head back home, along a different path. When we got home, we spend some time in recovery. A little while later, my kids ask me if they could take a walk down that path so that they could see the waterfall. Should I let them?"
Do you know what most people have told me? "No!!"
"Well, why not?" I ask.
"Because of the many dangers that were on the path!" They exclaim.

Cross Words – Week 7 - EVIL

"Exactly!" I resound. "That is why we as parents do not want you do go down the paths that were hazardous for us. Yes we survived the dangers, but the effects they had on us still linger with us today."

The story makes a dramatic understanding of the pitfalls that Satan puts in our way, and that we should desire to never go down the wrong paths ever again. Even though we may feel strong enough, we will fail, if we aren't relying on God.

Keep in mind, though the enemy lurks behind every corner... those intentions are all in vain! We, who are committed to Christ, have a wonderful reassurance of having the best guide and "bodyguard" through the trials. Scripture tells us what the punishment will be for the enemy in the end.

Revelation 20:1-3;7, 9-10

> *[1] And I saw an angel coming down out of heaven, having the key to the Abyss and holding in his hand a great chain. [2] He seized the dragon, that ancient serpent, who is the devil, or Satan, and bound him for a thousand years. [3] He threw him into the Abyss, and locked and sealed it over him, to keep him from deceiving the nations anymore until the thousand years were ended. After that, he must*

Cross Words – Week 7 - EVIL

be set free for a short time.
[7] When the thousand years are over, Satan will be released from his prison... [9] They marched across the breadth of the earth and surrounded the camp of God's people, the city he loves. But fire came down from heaven and devoured them. [10] And the devil, who deceived them, was thrown into the lake of burning sulfur, where the beast and the false prophet had been thrown. They will be tormented day and night for ever and ever.

- ❖ Don't give in to the ways of the **EVIL** one!

- ❖ What in your life may be allowing the Enemy's Vain Intentions to Lurk? Are there things that you watch or listen to that open the door to your heart to the enemy?

- ❖ God is in control, even over the enemy. Trust in God and He will save you.

- ❖ This week, pray the last words of the "Lords Prayer" daily – "Lead us not into temptations, but deliver us from the **EVIL** one. For thine is the kingdom, the power, and the glory, both now and forevermore."

Cross Words – Week 7 - EVIL

PRAYER

Father, I praise and thank you for the power and authority you have over the forces of EVIL. Strengthen me so that I will be able to withstand the attacks of the enemy. I cannot do this alone. I must rely on your Sovereign grace and power. Though we do not understand why EVIL has become so rampant in this world, we know that you will have the final say. I pray for those who are feeling the effects of the enemy today. Send your angels to guard and protect them. Deliver us, O Lord, from the power of the Evil one! Amen.

Cross Words – Week 7 - LUST

LUST

Living Under Satan's Traps

1 John 2:16, 17;

> *⁶ For everything in the world--the cravings of sinful man, the <u>lust</u> of his eyes and the boasting of what he has and does--comes not from the Father but from the world. ¹⁷ The world and its desires pass away, but the man who does the will of God lives forever.*

Many think that lust only has to do with how a man or a woman is attracted to the other in sexually desirable way. However, lust is merely the intense desire of someone or something so much that you just have to have it, whether physically or mentally.

Some lust after people, some after clothes, still others lust after cars, money, etc. As the acronym states, these are all just traps that Satan puts in our way. Why would you want to live under his traps? Especially when you know it is he who puts them in our way to cause us to stumble. Avoid the traps at all costs!

I had the opportunity to see this concept visualized as I spent

Cross Words – Week 7 - LUST

time with my son at a Cub scouts' Camp. There were some teenage boys who were attempting to set a snare up in a tree to catch passersby. I looked up, saw the trap and said. "Now don't you think it would be foolish if I just walked under this snare?"

They responded, "Yeah, but that's the whole idea." That is when I decided to share with them the **LUST** acronym.

I continued with, "If I step into this area, you could ensnare me and then have control over me, right?" That's the same way that **LUST** affects us; Satan lures us into an area that seems safe (an affair for example), and even wonderful (lots of money). Then without warning, we are trapped! The reason I avoided the boy's snare was because I was looking up. Keep your eyes focused on the things above so you will see the snares ahead, and immediately flee the area.

James 4:7,8;

> *⁴ "Submit yourselves, then, to God. Resist the devil, and he will flee from you. ⁸ Come near to God and He will come near to you."*

(To get the full meaning of these verses begin reading from James 1:1.)

Many people have fallen prey to the traps of Satan. One of

Cross Words – Week 7 - LUST

these traps, in particular, is the *L.U.S.T.* after others. An extremely volatile industry of the 20th and 21st Centuries is the display of pornography, in all its forms. It is a very sad day when we have cheapened a God-given blessing to something meaningless and abused. It has become even more convenient for people to access such material. The Internet is filled with such filth! People have fallen into these traps, not realizing all the consequences because of it.

There are many serious scams involved with connecting to these sites. Moreover, think of how you are allowing this trash to enter your home and mind. No, you are not actually making love to this person on the computer, but you become connected or one with the person, spiritually. I beg of you, please do not allow yourself to suffer in this pit of despair that actually prevents us from having a Spiritual intimacy with Jesus, and proper physical intimacy with our spouse.

If necessary, get help from a Christian specialist, or call 1-800-NEW-LIFE to arrange for contact with a specialist through New Life ministries. Founder, Steve Arterburn, and Fred Stoeker wrote a book called *Every Man's Battle*. I found this

Cross Words – Week 7 - LUST

book to be powerful and enabled me to find true purity. In it Steve states:

> *You're in a tough position.*
> *You live in a world awash with sensual images available twenty-four hours a day in a variety of mediums: print, television, videos, the Internet---even phones.*
>
> *But God offers you freedom from the slavery of sin through the cross of Christ, and He created your eyes and mind with an ability to be trained and controlled.*
> *We simply have to stand up and walk by His power in the right path. Men need a battle plan a detailed plan for becoming a man of sexual integrity.*

Yes, the Internet is full of such filth, but as men we must also train our eyes and minds to focus away from lusting after women that we encounter everyday. The number of affairs that couples are involved in is growing, and it may not even be a physical relationship – merely intellectual or emotional. Again, to LUST is to desire something or someone we cannot have. I have heard the saying, "The grass is always greener on the other side of the fence.", but we must not end this saying here,

Cross Words – Week 7 - LUST

for there is an important ending to it – ", but we have to mow it there also." In other words, though the other person seems appealing, there will still have to be areas that have to be worked out with them as well.

A good way to stop such foolish relationships is to **never** start any! If you are married, tell the other person about your spouse and how much you love your spouse. If it appears to be flirtatious, identify it, correct it, and then leave at a high rate of speed. Don't become trapped by Satan's lures. If you are not married, this does not give you license to "play the field"; you still need to keep yourself pure until the wedding day. Don't destroy someone else's life by LUSTing after someone else's spouse.

> Christ says in **Matthew 5:27-28;**
>
> *[27] "You have heard that it was said, `Do not commit adultery.' [28] But I tell you that anyone who looks at a woman lustfully has already committed adultery with her in his heart."*

This is one area that God had to do some major work on me. In fact, I believe it may have been a good reason why my marriage failed. I have finally learned my lesson!

Cross Words – Week 7 - LUST

Furthermore, since you become spiritually connected to that person, you actually break the bond of your marriage. This is true, whether for a man or a woman. On the wedding day, God made you no longer two, but one – what effects one also affects the other.

Genesis 2:24;

> *"For this reason a man will leave his father and mother and be united to his wife, and they will become one flesh."*

❖ Are you being lured into the enemy's traps?

❖ If you feel that **LUST** has its control on you, find ways to flee from it.

❖ God can and will help you to see the trap so you can avoid it.

Cross Words – Week 7 - LUST

PRAYER

Father, open my eyes that I might see the traps that the Satan has put to Trap me. I need your help to avoid them. If there are areas now that I have been ensnared by the enemy in, please help me to be free of them by releasing them to you. I want live a life that is pure and holy, set apart for you. Amen.

Week 8

<u>HOLY</u>

Is your life yielded to God?

HOLY – **H**aving **O**ur **L**ives **Y**ielded

OBEY – **O**rder **B**y **E**veryday **Y**ielding

WORD – **W**ay **O**f **R**efreshing **D**aily

ZEAL – **Z**estful **E**nthusiasm **A**bout **L**ife

Cross Words – Week 8 - HOLY

HOLY
Have Our Lives Yielded

Jude 1:20,21;

> [20] But you, dear friends, build yourselves up in your most <u>holy</u> faith and pray in the Holy Spirit. [21] Keep yourselves in God's love as you wait for the mercy of our Lord Jesus Christ to bring you to eternal life.

I had heard a speaker at a men's conference some years ago, compare holiness to a toothbrush. He explained that on his honeymoon, his wife had forgotten to bring her own toothbrush, so she kindly asked him if she could use his. He flat out said, "No!" "Why?" she cried. "We kiss each other, so what's the difference?"

"Because this toothbrush is for my mouth only!"

That is how we are to be with God, to be set apart for Him. Yielding our souls only to Him.

I Peter 1: 15,16;

> [15] "But just as he who called you is holy, so be holy in all that you do; [16] or it is written: "Be holy, because I am holy."

Cross Words – Week 8 - HOLY

- ❖ Have you yielded your life to God?
- ❖ Being holy doesn't have to be chore, rather a privilege
- ❖ This week, focus on setting yourself apart only for God.

PRAYER

Father, I want to be holy, just as you are holy. Help me to yield my life to you each day. I want to be set apart for you only. The things of this life tend to distract or corrupt me, but I know that you will give me the strength and desire to remain in your will. I love you. Amen.

Cross Words – Week 8 - OBEY

OBEY

Order By Everyday Yielding

Matthew 8:27;

> *"What kind of man is this? Even the winds and the waves <u>obey</u> Him!"*

We should desire to live a life that is PURE and HOLY – set apart for our Heavenly Father by OBEYing Him. If we set the goal each morning to have our lives yielded to God, and decide (resolve) to live everyday in a perfect and untainted way, we will have victory!

As parents, we want our children to OBEY. Why? Because if they will yield to our experience and authority, there may be some order to our day, and thus we will all have peace and fulfillment.

Colossians 3:20;

> [20] *Children, obey your parents in everything, for this pleases the Lord.*

Cross Words – Week 8 - OBEY

Ephesians 6:1-3;

> [1] *Children, obey your parents in the Lord, for this is right.* [2] *"Honor your father and mother"--which is the first commandment with a promise--* [3] *"that it may go well with you and that you may enjoy long life on the earth."*

To force someone to obey merely develops a "mindless slave", and that is not how God is with us. He provides us with free will; meaning that though He disciplines like a father, He gives us the choice of whether or not to follow Him. When we, as parents, raise up the standard for our children, help them learn from their mistakes, and yet allow them, when they are old enough, to decide for themselves, they will become better people. I have heard said that "Rules without Relationship lead to Rebellion".

- ❖ Do you want more order in your life?

- ❖ Are you willing to yield your life to others, especially God?

- ❖ This week, think upon the song,
    - o "Trust and Obey" –
  by John H. Sammis and Daniel B. Towner
  "Trust and obey, for there's no other way to be happy in Jesus, But to trust and obey."

Cross Words – Week 8 - OBEY

PRAYER

Father, in you alone will I Trust and OBEY. I desire to have more order to my life, and through obeying you I will develop this in my life. Help me to OBEY others of authority in my life. I want to find the peace that comes only when I learn to OBEY you. Amen.

Cross Words – Week 8 - WORD

WORD
Way **O**f **R**efreshing **D**aily

John 1:14;
> "The Word became flesh and made his dwelling among us. We have seen his glory, the glory of the One and Only, who came from the Father, full of grace and truth."

When Satan tempted Christ, Jesus didn't yell at him, fight with him, or even argue with him. He did, however, use the WORD of God to challenge Satan. Each time He was tempted, He would quote the Scriptures, throwing Satan off.

Matthew 4:1-11;
> [1] Then Jesus was led by the Spirit into the desert to be tempted by the devil. [2] After fasting forty days and forty nights, he was hungry. [3] The tempter came to him and said, "If you are the Son of God, tell these stones to become bread." [4] Jesus answered, "It is written: `Man does not live on bread alone, but on every word that comes from the mouth of God.' " [5] Then the devil took him to the holy city and had him stand on the highest point of the temple. [6] "If you are the Son of God," he said, "throw yourself down. For it is written: " `He will command his angels concerning you, and they will lift you up in their

> *hands, so that you will not strike your foot against a stone.' "* [7] *Jesus answered him, "<u>It is also written</u>: `Do not put the Lord your God to the test.' "* [8] *Again, the devil took him to a very high mountain and showed him all the kingdoms of the world and their splendor.* [9] *"All this I will give you," he said, "if you will bow down and worship me."* [10] *Jesus said to him, "Away from me, Satan! <u>For it is written</u>: `Worship the Lord your God, and serve him only.' "* [11] *Then the devil left him, and angels came and attended him.*

Have you ever been in a desert? It is very hot and dry, and at times your mind can play tricks on you like a mirage. The only thing that helps the weary traveler continue is to get in the shade and get some cool water to be refreshed. In verse 11, the angels came to provide Jesus refreshment. The word of God is also a source of refreshing daily. It teaches and encourages us, and, from the account of Jesus' temptation, it defends us.

I urge you to begin immediately to read and memorize Scripture, that you may have the right Word to speak against the enemy. I can't tell you the countless times that God has spoken to me directly through the Word.

Hebrews 4:12;

> *"For the word of God is living and active. Sharper than any double-edged sword, it penetrates even to dividing*

Cross Words – Week 8 - WORD

soul and spirit, joints and marrow; it judges the thoughts and attitudes of the heart."

❖ Do you need some refreshing in your life?

❖ Do you have a Bible? If not, I encourage you to get one.

❖ Some people have a Bible, yet they just leave it on their table, for looks. What if we compare this to having a nice shiny red apple on the table: Every day, we admire how red and shiny it is and even show our friends how big it is, yet never actually take a bite of it! What good is the apple unless we actually take a bite of it! The true nourishment comes when we feed on it until we get to the core.

❖ If possible, join a Bible study.

❖ Feed on His WORD, that you might have life within you

❖ Begin to memorize Scripture so that you may be wise and give an accurate account when asked. A friend of mine, Timothy, showed me one way to memorize by taking the first letter of each word and focus on it alone to remember the word. For example John 3:16 states "For God so loved the world, that He gave His only begotten Son, that whosoever believes in Him shall not perish but have everlasting life." To memorize this, write down:

John 3:16; F G s l t w, t H g H o b S, t w b i H s n p b h e l.

Cross Words – Week 8 - WORD

PRAYER

*Father, I thank you for your Word is alive and true. I pray that "I have hidden your Word in my heart, that I might not sin against you." (Psalm 119:11) As I begin to study your Word, speak to me and refresh me. I know it will lead and guide me. "Thy Word is a lamp unto my feet and a light unto my path" (*Psalm 119:105) *When the enemy presses in, help me to recall the Words of Scripture to thwart his plans. I love you. Amen.*

Cross Words – Week 8 - ZEAL

ZEAL
Zestful Enthusiasm About Life

Romans 12:11-13;

> [11] Never be lacking in zeal, but keep your spiritual fervor, serving the Lord. [12] Be joyful in hope, patient in affliction, faithful in prayer. [13] Share with God's people who are in need. Practice hospitality.

It is great to have ZEAL in our life; it is what drives some people to start their day. It is what keeps our heart focused on the right ways. To have ZEAL for the Lord is to have a true devoted heart.

However, Paul states in **Romans 10:2-4;**

> [2] For I can testify about them that they are zealous for God, but their zeal is not based on knowledge. [3] Since they did not know the righteousness that comes from God and sought to establish their own, they did not submit to God's righteousness. [4] Christ is the end of the law so that there may be righteousness for everyone who believes.

Thus, one can have ZEAL for the Lord and not have had any knowledge of Him! What an incredibly merciful and loving

Cross Words – Week 8 - ZEAL

God we serve.

- ❖ Do you have a Zestful Enthusiasm About Life?
- ❖ What are other types of ZEAL?
- ❖ When we have a close relationship with the Lord, we will have much more Enthusiasm About Life.

PRAYER

Father, I pray that I will always have a ZEAL for you and this life you have given me. With this Enthusiasm, help me to show others of your wondrous plan for their lives. I now have a reason to live! Amen.

Week 9

CARE

How do you show people that they are loved?

CARE – **C**onsider **A**nother **R**egarding **E**verything

SMILE – **S**how **M**otivation **I**nto **L**ives **E**veryday

GIVE – **G**enerosity **I**s **V**ery **E**ncouraging

HUG – **H**old **U**s **G**ently

Cross Words – Week 9 - CARE

CARE
Consider Another Regarding Everything

John 21:16,
> *Again Jesus said, "Simon son of John, do you truly love me?" He answered, "Yes, Lord, you know that I love you." Jesus said, "Take <u>care</u> of my sheep."*

I care a lot about my family; I **CARE** about every aspect of their lives, what they will eat, wear, sleep, friends, etc. I consider it not only my responsibility, but also my privilege.

To **CARE** for someone or something does have its rewards: the recipient benefits by knowing that their life is important to someone, and the giver benefits by knowing they have enabled someone to grow and have security.

It is so disheartening that so many people, including parents, use the expression, "I Don't Care." even when the child is just asking if they can go over to a friend's house. If only we would listen to what we are saying!

Cross Words – Week 9 - CARE

An example of **CARE** in action is the familiar story of the "Good Samaritan".

Luke 10:30-37;

> [30] In reply Jesus said: "A man was going down from Jerusalem to Jericho, when he fell into the hands of robbers. They stripped him of his clothes, beat him and went away, leaving him half dead. [31] A priest happened to be going down the same road, and when he saw the man, he passed by on the other side. [32] So too, a Levite, when he came to the place and saw him, passed by on the other side. [33] But a Samaritan, as he traveled, came where the man was; and when he saw him, he took pity on him. [34] He went to him and bandaged his wounds, pouring on oil and wine. Then he put the man on his own donkey, took him to an inn and took care of him. [35] The next day he took out two silver coins and gave them to the innkeeper. `Look after him,' he said, `and when I return, I will reimburse you for any extra expense you may have.' [36] "Which of these three do you think was a neighbor to the man who fell into the hands of robbers?" [37] The expert in the law replied, "The one who had mercy on him." Jesus told him, "Go and do likewise."

It is not because of the good man's righteousness that Christ acknowledges him, rather, because of his kindness and compassion. He cared for the poor, beaten traveler, that no one would help, and the Jewish people considered this good man an outsider.

Cross Words – Week 9 - CARE

Did the ones who were supposedly the "right" people to give care provide it? Did the one who was considered an outcast neglect to care for his beaten oppressor? The answer to both questions is No. The religious leaders, who had taught God's love and compassion, did not show it to one of their own. Furthermore, the Samaritan cared for the man above and beyond what would be deemed adequate.

Consider the acronym *C.A.R.E.* again; in it God asks us to **C**onsider "**A**nother" **R**egarding "**E**verything". This means we must consider helping those we may find less than desirable: the convict, the homeless, the drunkard, or the person of another culture that we don't understand. The "another" refers to anyone or anything other than us, and "everything" is quite self-explanatory. Nurses, doctors, hospice workers, animal rescue centers, teachers, and others that are compassionate, continually take "**CARE**" to the fullest.

If you consider another person regarding everything in their life, you are actually caring for them. They need you, and you are given the opportunity to help.

Cross Words – Week 9 - CARE

- Do you take **CARE** of the people/things that are in your life?

- ❖ In what ways could you show others how much you **CARE** about them?

- ❖ Jesus **CARE**s for you so much that He gave up His own life, so that yours could be saved.

- ❖ Take time today to take **CARE** of someone/something.

PRAYER

Father, thank you for all the LOVE and CARE that you provide me. Help me to Consider Another Regarding Everything, even when I would rather not. Amen.

Cross Words – Week 9 - SMILE

SMILE

Show **M**otivation **I**nto **L**ives **E**veryday

Job 9:27

> [27] *If I say, `I will forget my complaint,
> I will change my expression, and <u>smile</u>,*

By giving someone a **SMILE**, we are enabling them to see how much we care, thus motivating them to go on. A genuine smile can break the saddest heart; it can give them the reason to go on. Someone once asked me, "As a Funeral Director, what's the best thing you ever told a grieving family member?" I replied, "Nothing. Just **SMILE** and let them know that you're there for them. Words tend to get us into trouble; we could say the wrong thing, or say something nice like 'I'll visit you soon!' and not follow through with it. Just be there!"

A **SMILE** is a universal sign of friendliness. Whether you're in the United States or in Africa, a smile will communicate an understanding when words cannot be expressed.

Cross Words – Week 9 - SMILE

We need to start providing more care to those around us, and again, this will put faith into action. We are Christ's hands and feet upon this earth, and we show His love and compassion by our acts of love.

1 John 3: 18-20;

> [18] Dear children, let us not love with words or tongue but with actions and in truth. [19] This then is how we know that we belong to the truth, and how we set our hearts at rest in his presence [20] whenever our hearts condemn us. For God is greater than our hearts, and he knows everything.

- ❖ Right now, just smile. Look at yourself. Don't you feel happier?

- ❖ You can Motivate someone with such a simple expression.

- ❖ This week, try this: SMILE at more people than you have before. What are their responses?

PRAYER

Father, you give me every reason to SMILE, you Motivate me even in my darkest hour. When I am down, I know that you will pick me up, everyday. Help me to Motivate others by giving them a SMILE. I love you. Amen.

Cross Words – Week 9 - GIVE

GIVE

Generosity **I**s **V**ery **E**ncouraging

Romans 12:8;

> *⁸ if it is encouraging, let him encourage; if it is contributing to the needs of others, let him give generously; if it is leadership, let him govern diligently; if it is showing mercy, let him do it cheerfully.*

When you **GIVE**, you are not only encouraging the recipient of the gift, but also, yourself. Yes, yourself! Because God loves a cheerful giver, and giving opens a floodgate of joy within you. God wants us to give Him our all.

Deuteronomy 6:5;

> *"Love the LORD your God with all your heart and with all your soul and with all your strength."*

Or as I heard it interpreted by a pastor; *"Love the Lord your God with all your passion, intellect, prayer, and power."*

He wants us to not be concerned about the mundane things in our lives. He wants us to be willing to lose our life, for Him. And, by giving of ourselves to others, we are fulfilling God's commission to us – to "go out into the world and make

Cross Words – Week 9 - GIVE

disciples of all people, baptizing them in the name of the Father, the Son, and Holy Spirit." Faith is not something that can be contained; it must be passed on. If you have ever played a game of "hot potato", you know that you can't keep the potato in your hand for very long. It will cause you to lose the game.

Mark 8: 34-38;

> [34] Then he called the crowd to him along with his disciples and said: "If anyone would come after me, he must deny himself and take up his cross and follow me. [35] For whoever wants to save his life will lose it, but whoever loses his life for me and for the gospel will save it. [36] What good is it for a man to gain the whole world, yet forfeit his soul? [37] Or what can a man give in exchange for his soul? [38] If anyone is ashamed of me and my words in this adulterous and sinful generation, the Son of Man will be ashamed of him when he comes in his Father's glory with the holy angels."

The Ray Boltz song **"Thank you"** says, "Thank you for giving to the Lord, I am life that was changed. I am so glad you gave."

The song also talks of seeing these people in heaven. The lives of those we may have touched throughout our life here, whether directly or indirectly. Plant the seeds – you don't know when those seeds will grow, but they will grow!

Investing our time and resources on others is crucial to faith. We can either invest wisely and reap a great reward, or we can simply settle into the faith we already have and hoard it. A chilling reminder of this is in:

Matthew 25:14-30;

> [14] "Again, it will be like a man going on a journey, who called his servants and entrusted his property to them. [15] To one he gave five talents of money, to another two talents, and to another one talent, each according to his ability. Then he went on his journey. [16] The man who had received the five talents went at once and put his money to work and gained five more. [17] So also, the one with the two talents gained two more. [18] But the man who had received the one talent went off, dug a hole in the ground and hid his master's money. [19] "After a long time the master of those servants returned and settled accounts with them. [20] The man who had received the five talents brought the other five. `Master,' he said, `you entrusted me with five talents. See, I have gained five more.' [21] "His master replied, `Well done, good and faithful servant! You have been faithful with a few things; I will put you in charge of many things. Come and share your master's happiness!' [22] "The man with the two talents also came. `Master,' he said, `you entrusted me with two talents; see, I have gained two more.' [23] "His master replied, `Well done, good and faithful servant! You have been faithful with a few things; I will put you in charge of many things.

Cross Words – Week 9 - GIVE

Come and share your master's happiness!" [24] "Then the man who had received the one talent came. `Master,' he said, `I knew that you are a hard man, harvesting where you have not sown and gathering where you have not scattered seed. [25] So I was afraid and went out and hid your talent in the ground. See, here is what belongs to you.'
[26] "His master replied, `You wicked, lazy servant! So you knew that I harvest where I have not sown and gather where I have not scattered seed? [27] Well then, you should have put my money on deposit with the bankers, so that when I returned I would have received it back with interest. : [28] " `Take the talent from him and give it to the one who has the ten talents. [29] For everyone who has will be given more, and he will have abundance. Whoever does not have, even what he has will be taken from him. [30] And throw that worthless servant outside, into the darkness, where there will be weeping and gnashing of teeth.'

The one who had invested his talents, received an incredible return on his investment, yet the one who hoarded it was left with nothing. Get out there and invest your time and talents, and resources to win souls! The time is now! Especially when the rate of interest is so high! That is to say, people are more open to hear the Word of God, especially with all the wars and rumors of wars. Keep in mind, though, people want to be talked to, and cared about, not preached to.

Cross Words – Week 9 - GIVE

❖ Do you consider yourself a "cheerful giver"?

❖ Do you realize the gifts that God has given you?

❖ This week, take time to give of yourself for others. You will be greatly encouraged as well.

PRAYER

Father, you gave the greatest gift of all – your Son, Jesus, that we might have life and that more abundantly. Help me to give of myself, whether it is with time, prayer, or money. I desire to encourage others so that they too might know You and have eternal life. Help me to use the gifts You have given me to invest in others. Amen.

Cross Words – Week 9 - HUG

HUG
Hold **U**s **G**ently

Ecclesiastes 3:5

a time to embrace and a time to refrain,

A very simple act of love can be a gentle **HUG**. It stimulates the body and is beneficial to the one being hugged and the hugger. Hugging an animal, blanket, etc. can have similar results, but people are much better. However, I don't recommend you try hugging a porcupine; if you get my point.

I love giving hugs, especially to a group of "young" ladies (65 years old or more) in my church. They actually look forward to their morning **HUG**, and it gives me another good reason to get myself to church. But my hugs are for anyone who will receive them, especially when someone is hurting.

Bill is a man in our church that became well-known, not because of some great, amazing feat, rather because he is a wonderful greeter and friend. He will greet everyone that enters the church with a smile and a hug. The women get a gentle **HUG**, and the men get "reeled-in" for a **HUG**. They

Cross Words – Week 9 - HUG

will sometimes resist the **HUG**, because they feel they don't need one, and then they accept the **HUG** and feel better for it.

Recommended reading:

Hugs for the hurting

Stories by John William Smith and Personalized Scriptures by LeAnn Weiss

- ❖ Do you enjoy receiving hugs? If not, why do you think that is?
- ❖ There is a saying, "Some things are better left unsaid", and hugs can say much more than words could ever.
- ❖ This week, take time to **HUG** as many people as you can.
  - o How did it make them feel?
  - o How did it make you feel?

PRAYER

Father, I thank You that I can feel secure in Your Everlasting arms. When you Hold Us Gently, we can deal with anything, knowing how much You love us. When someone else is hurting, help me to show others how much I care through this simple act of love. Amen.

Cross Words – Week 10

Week 10

FORGIVE

Are you willing let go and let God?

PAST – **P**ut **A**side **S**hadowed **T**imes

PRIDE – **P**utting **R**ationale **I**nto **D**ecisions **E**veryday

--**P**utting **R**esponsibility **I**n **D**oing **E**verything

SORRY – **S**howing **O**ur **R**emorse **R**estores **Y**ou

FORGIVE –

Finding **O**ur **R**elationship **G**row **I**s **V**ery **E**ncouraging

Cross Words – Week 10 - PAST

PAST
Put Aside Shadowed Times

Isaiah 43:18;

"Forget the former things; do not dwell on the past."

Asking ourselves if we really want to get well empowers us to find true healing in Jesus through faith and persistence. We need to be healed of any difficulties in our PAST by finding every opportunity to FORGIVE those who have harmed us. Furthermore, our ultimate healing will be when we are face to face before our Lord and Savior.

I saw a Christian T-shirt printed with:

> **"When the devil reminds you of your past, remind him of his future!"**

By Carmen (the singer).

There are many things from my PAST that attempt to haunt me, times that were shadowed (darkened). However, if I don't put them aside, I cannot continue on my walk. Much like

Cross Words – Week 10 - PAST

trying to climb a mountain with a 500-pound sack of diamonds and rocks on your back; though it probably could be done, what use are the precious diamonds (which amount to about a pound in the sack) in the first place if you can't get to your destination- the top? Lighten the load by getting rid of the unnecessary things you cling to and get climbing!

Or, imagine a beautiful sailboat, with all the greatest equipment and sails, geared for taking on any lake or ocean, yet it is held back because you won't release the anchor from the dock. Sail on! Release yourself from your PAST and be free to sail into the future!

Matthew 11:30;

"For my yoke is easy and my burden is light."

He never said that we wouldn't have burdens in this life. He did say, however, that His burden is light.

"Give them all to Jesus and He will turn your sorrows into joy." --Evie

Cross Words – Week 10 - PAST

- Has holding onto your past done you any good?

- Put Aside those things in your life that haunt you, and live.

- I saw a fascinating plaque that has helped me immensely:
  - **"Live each day as though Jesus died yesterday, rose today and is coming back tomorrow.**

- This week, gradually look at those areas of your past and let them go, through God's help. If necessary, find a good counselor that will help you focus on the healing that God can bring as you let go.

PRAYER

Father, thank you that you love me so much that you sent Jesus to take care of the areas of my PAST. You are the God of Yesterday, Today, and Forever. Jesus, the past haunts me at times, and it is difficult to bear. I pray that you will help me to let go of those areas so that you can help me to live the life You have chosen for me. I cannot do this without You. Today, I will begin to let it all go. Amen.

Cross Words – Week 10 - PRIDE

PRIDE

Putting **R**esponsibility **I**n **D**oing **E**verything

Putting **R**ationale **I**nto **D**ecisions **E**veryday

2 Corinthians 7:4;

> [4] *I have great confidence in you; I take great <u>pride</u> in you. I am greatly encouraged; in all our troubles my joy knows no bounds.*

I have great pride in my children. Why? Because they are all gifts from God. They are beautiful, talented children, and God has given me and their mother the responsibility of caring for their needs.

This is when we are **P**utting **R**esponsibility **I**n **D**oing **E**verything.

Maybe you think, "I'm not going to admit my guilt, I have too much pride!" That may be the very reason you are struggling with your burden.

I have heard someone say, "I don't do dishes, I have too much pride!" This is when we are using rationale to explain why we

Cross Words – Week 10 - PRIDE

feel the way we do.

Proverbs 11:12;

> *"When <u>pride</u> comes, then comes disgrace, but with humility comes wisdom."*

James 1:9-11;

> *[9] The brother in humble circumstances ought to take <u>pride</u> in his high position. [10] But the one who is rich should take <u>pride</u> in his low position, because he will pass away like a wild flower. [11] For the sun rises with scorching heat and withers the plant; its blossom falls and its beauty is destroyed. In the same way, the rich man will fade away even while he goes about his business.*

Pride can be the very thing that lifts us up and gives us purpose, or it can drag us down to utter disgrace. Consider the last two Scriptures – each one is asking us to humble ourselves and be more content with what we have. Both myself and Scripture are not saying that being rich is wrong; however, riches can cause us to lose sight of our dependency on the Lord.

Cross Words – Week 10 - PRIDE

- ❖ Are you taking your responsibilities seriously?
- ❖ Or are you rationalizing why you do what you do?
- ❖ This week, take time to put some PRIDE in your family and work, while letting go of your rationale.

PRAYER

Father, I thank You for how much PRIDE you have in your children. I ask you today to help me take responsibility for the things in my life. Please help me not to rationalize and be caught up in my own ego that I lose sight of you. Help me to be humble. Amen.

SORRY

Showing Our Remorse Restores You

2 Corinthians 7:8-13;

> [8] *Even if I caused you sorrow by my letter, I do not regret it. Though I did regret it--I see that my letter hurt you, but only for a little while--* [9] *yet now I am happy, not because you were made <u>sorry</u>, but because your sorrow led you to repentance. For you became sorrowful as God intended and so were not harmed in any way by us.* [10] *Godly sorrow brings repentance that leads to salvation and leaves no regret, but worldly sorrow brings death.* [11] *See what this godly sorrow has produced in you: what earnestness, what eagerness to clear yourselves, what indignation, what alarm, what longing, what concern, what readiness to see justice done. At every point you have proved yourselves to be innocent in this matter.* [12] *So even though I wrote to you, it was not on account of the one who did the wrong or of the injured party, but rather that before God you could see for yourselves how devoted to us you are.* [13] *By all this we are encouraged.*

When you truly show your remorse for a wrongdoing, the offended person is much more likely to allow the relationship to be restored. Now, this doesn't mean that every time we say we are sorry that we should be immediately restored. No!

Cross Words – Week 10 - SORRY

The condition is the true remorse shown to the other. I know I have asked my kids to say they are sorry to each other, and they usually say it in such a way that it sounds forced.

This only makes the situation worse. To show remorse is to admit fault and be willing to change.

- ❖ What areas of your life do you need to be sorry for?
- ❖ Have you shown true Remorse for your faults?
- ❖ When is someone truly **SORRY** for what they've done?
- ❖ Have you told Jesus that you are **SORRY**?
- ❖ This week, go to those you may have offended and let them know how **SORRY** you are. Your life will be changed.

PRAYER

Father, I am SORRY for my sins. I accept Jesus' gift of grace for my life. Help me to show others how SORRY I am for offending them, but also accept their apology when they offend me. Only by your grace can this be done. Amen.

Cross Words – Week 10 - FORGIVE

FORGIVE

Finding **O**ur **R**elationship **G**row **I**s **V**ery **E**ncouraging

Matthew 6:12, 14-15;

> Jesus says, [12] "*Forgive* us our debts, as we also have forgiven our debtors. [14] For if you *forgive* men when they sin against you, your heavenly Father will also *forgive* you. [15] But if you do not *forgive* men their sins, your Father will not *forgive* your sins."

Psalm 79:9;

> "Help us, O God our Savior, for the glory of your name; deliver us and forgive our sins for your name's sake."

When God forgives us, He completely forgets about that offense- never to be brought up ever again. He wants our relationship with Him to grow. He wants us to have peace, not frustration and pain. Wouldn't it be nice to see our relationships with others grow, rather than fail due to unresolved bitterness.

How many times is good enough to forgive someone? The Apostle Peter asked Jesus this very question. He thought that

Cross Words – Week 10 - FORGIVE

seven times would be sufficient, but Jesus had better intentions.

Matthew 18:21,22;

²¹ Then Peter came to Jesus and asked, "Lord, how many times shall I forgive my brother when he sins against me? Up to seven times?" ²² Jesus answered, "I tell you, not seven times, but seventy-seven times."

Jesus wants us not to even think about the number of times we **FORGIVE** someone. In the period that Jesus walked on the earth, seventy was consider a number of great magnitude, and seven was consider the perfect number. After all, God created the world in seven days. I have also heard it said as 70 X 7 times, in other words, 490 times! Furthermore, it is interesting to note that it is also mentioned in the Old Testament:

Genesis 4:24;

*"If Cain is avenged seven times,
then Lamech seventy-seven times."*

Get rid of any root of bitterness! It can only harm you. Holding in bitterness causes your body to not function as it should. Studies have shone that unresolved bitterness causes

Cross Words – Week 10 - FORGIVE

the body to react in adverse ways. It affects the immune system, the muscles, the heart, and the mind.

Our body is designed to work best under the best of conditions. Have you ever driven a car with just a little water in the gas-line? It causes the whole engine to work harder or not at all. Then we have to put in isopropyl alcohol to dry up or remove any water in the line. Christ came that we might have life and that to the fullest.

He wants us to live with our hearts, minds, and bodies at full potential.

God can heal us, but we need to first cleanse ourselves of the things that have contaminated us. Consider a surgeon in a hospital; we must first reveal to the doctor that something is bothering us; the doctor helps us discover the problem, and tells us that we need surgery. The doctors then go to wash themselves and the patient before the surgery. Why? To insure that no other contamination by bacteria can get into the extremely vulnerable area. The doctor removes the problem, through surgery, yet there is usually pain, even after the surgery. Furthermore, the doctor usually makes recommendations for a change of lifestyle.

Cross Words – Week 10 - FORGIVE

God is like that surgeon, He can and will heal us. We must trust that He is in control! Whether we are healed or whether we carry this until we die, we must be at peace either way.

I would like to take a moment to deal with forgiveness in my life. To those who have ever hurt or offended me, consider yourself forgiven. To those whom I have hurt, either purposefully or unintentionally, I humbly ask for your forgiveness. There are friends and family that I would truly love to become reacquainted with, if only the relationships could be reconciled. Most of all, I ask my Savior, Jesus Christ, to forgive me of my many sins. I would truly like to see my relationships grow, and I don't want anything to prevent that.

- ❖ Do you want your relationships to grow?
- ❖ Do you wish to be forgiven by God?
- ❖ Are you willing to let go of your anger, bitterness, and pain, and have a new growth in your life? This only happens when we forgive.
- ❖ Ask others for their forgiveness.

Cross Words – Week 10 - FORGIVE

❖ This week, take time to **FORGIVE** those who have hurt you. I know it painful, but the healing will come after you do.

PRAYER

Father, I thank you that as I confess my sins to you, you will FORGIVE me – no matter how great or small the offense is. You have said, "As far as the east is from the west, so I have taken your sins from you" - My sins are blotted out of your book, when I ask for forgiveness. Wow! You are an amazingly wonderful and loving God! I desire to have my relationship with You and others to grow. I also know that your forgiveness is only as great as we forgive others. Help me to see Your grace, and forgive others. Amen.

Cross Words – Week 11

Week 11

TRUTH

What is truth?

TRUTH – **T**otally **R**ight **U**nderstanding **T**hrough **H**im

TRUST – **T**otal **R**eliance **U**nder **S**tressful **T**imes

WAY -- **W**alk **A**lways **Y**ielding

PRAISE –

Proclaiming **R**ighteous **A**cclamation **I**nspiring **S**omeone's **E**xcellence

Cross Words – Week 11 - TRUTH

TRUE

Totally Right Understanding Everyday

TRUTH

Totally Right Understanding Through Him

John 14:4-7;

> [4] *"You know the way to the place where I am going." [5] Thomas said to him, "Lord, we don't know where you are going, so how can we know the way?" [6] Jesus answered, "I am the way and the <u>truth</u> and the life. No one comes to the Father except through me. [7] If you really knew me, you would know my Father as well. From now on, you do know him and have seen him."*

John 8:31,32;

> [31] *"To the Jews who had believed him, Jesus said, "If you hold to my teaching, you are really my disciples. [32] Then you will know the <u>truth</u>, and the <u>truth</u> will set you free."*

Truth is a word that seems to be diced up by all sorts of different groups. "Truth is what ever you make it to be." "Is there really any real truth?" "Truth is just a concept that varies

Cross Words – Week 11 - TRUTH

from person to person."

However, the absolute truth comes from a Totally Right Understanding Through Him, not through anyone or anything else. Jesus explained, as mentioned in the above verse, that the key to understanding truth is to hold to His teachings. Where do we go to obtain this knowledge? The Word, of course.

It has been common practice in American courtrooms to put one's hand on the Bible and be asked, "Do you swear to tell the TRUTH, the whole TRUTH, and nothing but the TRUTH, so help you God?" To which you are to respond, "I do." This statement helps us to further understand the TRUTH acronym, because that is exactly what it means.

- ❖ What does TRUTH mean to you?
- ❖ Are you living a life that is based on Totally Right Understanding Through Him?
- ❖ What is the difference between a lie and the TRUTH?
- ❖ This week, concentrate on speaking and living the TRUTH in everything you do.

Cross Words – Week 11 - TRUTH

PRAYER

Father, I thank You that You are the Truth and that Your Word is TRUE. I pray that all I do is done based on your TRUTH. Help me to look to Your Word so that I may clearly understand the TRUTH. I know this world is mixed-up about the TRUTH, help me to always be an ambassador of the TRUTH. Amen.

Cross Words – Week 11 - TRUST

TRUST
Total Reliance Under Stressful Times

Faith begins in the wilderness – when you are alone and afraid, when things don't make sense… In the wilderness of loneliness we are terribly vulnerable… But we may be missing that fact that is hidden here… here we may learn to love Him – here, where it seems that He is not at work, where His will seems obscure or frightening, where He is not doing what we expected Him to do… If faith does not work here, in this situation, it will not work at all.
God's answer is always, "Trust Me."
by Elizabeth Elliot

In the story in **Matthew 7:24-27** (read it the ROCK chapter), think of the men who built their house and where they built it; the one who built his on sand relied on his own strength for security, and simply trusted that all would be without difficulty. However, the one who built his house on the solid foundation knew that he could trust that the rocks would withstand the storms so that they would not affect his home. Furthermore, the deeper he put his support beams into the rocks, the better he would be able to survive the storms. He totally relied on the rocks to support him during the stressful times of his life.

Cross Words – Week 11 - TRUST

Christ drove his support beam, the Cross, deep into the rocks of Calvary. And because of this, we know that we will withstand any storm in life. That is, of course, if we build our house on the foundation of Christ.

I believe that faith is a matter of totally relying on Christ at all times, not just the good times, but <u>all</u> times. I know, for myself, that it is not an easy task. Trusting in God is more than just believing in him; the demons believe in God, and even know that Jesus is the Son of God. However, they do not put their trust in him, nor do they rely on Him, and yet they know how to manipulate us to lose our trust in Jesus.

Proverbs 3:5-6;

> *⁵ <u>Trust</u> in the LORD with all your heart and lean not on your own understanding; ⁶ in all your ways acknowledge him, and he will make your paths straight.*

1 Corinthians 2:4-5;

> *⁴ My message and my preaching were not with wise and persuasive words, but with a demonstration of the Spirit's power, ⁵ so that your faith might not rest on men's wisdom, but on God's power.*

We must realize that it is not by our own power, nor by our

Cross Words – Week 11 - TRUST

own wisdom, rather, it is by God's power through the Holy Spirit. We cannot have faith if we are trusting in man's wisdom, furthermore, that would contradict our theme that we "Find Assurance In Trusting Him, not in men.

Believing is an essential beginning to having faith, however, learning to TRUST Christ, at all times, takes us to a whole new level of our spiritual walk.

We need to be able to totally rely on Christ for all our needs, daily. Even when our day seems like nothing could possibly go right. Think again of TRUST.

Children may grow up having difficulty trusting God, because their father here on earth has not been trustworthy. Dads, spend more quality time with your children than you do quantity of money on them.
Do you know how kids spell LOVE? ---T-I-M-E.

This is how you should spend your time with them:
- Spend time in prayer everyday for every member of your home.

Cross Words – Week 11 - TRUST

-Spend time playing a game with them, or just enjoy some time together.

-Spend time listening to their needs and problems in their life.

-Spend time sharing good and bad experiences you've had to strengthen them.

-Spend time teaching them the ways of this world. Do not leave it to others.

"Lord Give Me Time"
Author Unknown

Lord give me time to know a bit of peace,
Be free from care, before I grow too old,
Beyond the rainbow's end, may I at last,
Find where You've put my little pot of gold.
Lord, give me time to walk among the stars,
As fireflies flicker on a summer night,
Feel the fragile snowflakes on my face,
Hold Autumn to my heart in pure delight.

Lord, give me time to grow, that I may fit
The mold of what you wish me to become,
It is not easy for me, casting off
These human failings that I suffer from.
But faith has eyes much clearer than my own,
And Hope has wings to lift me up, and I'm
So full of Love, I know for sure I'm meant
For Heaven, given just a little time.

Cross Words – Week 11 - TRUST

If we expect the Heavenly Father to give us a little time, then it must be just as important for us to give children and others "a little time".

How are we to expect our children to trust their Heavenly Father, when we show no interest in their lives? Our children are desperately trying to get through to us. They don't need another swat, another yelling, or another silent treatment; they just need another hug, another encouragement, or a simple "I love you". Yes they do need to be disciplined, but they need most of all, to know they are loved. Don't take this role in life lightly! Help them trust their Heavenly Father through you.

- ❖ Do you fully trust and rely on God at all times? If not, when is it you find it hardest to trust him?

- ❖ Are you willing to put aside your own reservations to allow God to work? If not, what are some of your reservations? Ask Jesus to help you to let go of them so that you can be set free.

- ❖ Is it hard for you to trust others? If so, why do you think so?

- ❖ This week, focus on where you put your trust or the lack thereof.

Cross Words – Week 11 - TRUST

PRAYER

Father, I thank You that I can put my TRUST in You. I know that I can Totally Rely on you in the difficult times of my life. I shall give you my all, whether it is going great or when it is stressful. I know that as I "Trust in the Lord with all my heart, and lean not on my own understanding" You will "direct my paths". People tend to hurt us, but help me to be able to TRUST others again. Amen.

Cross Words – Week 11 - WAY

WAY
Walk Always Yielding

John 14:4-7;

> [4] *"You know the way to the place where I am going."* [5] *Thomas said to him, "Lord, we don't know where you are going, so how can we know the way?"* [6] *Jesus answered, "I am the way and the truth and the life. No one comes to the Father except through me.* [7] *If you really knew me, you would know my Father as well. From now on, you do know him and have seen him."*

There is a right WAY and a wrong WAY. If you ever drove down a One Way or the Wrong Way on a highway, you'll immediately notice that something isn't right, especially with all the oncoming cars!

Proverbs 14:12;

> *"There is a way that seems right to a man, but in the end it leads to death."*

The early Christians were known as "Followers of the Way"; since Jesus had provided the Way, they wanted to follow that path.

Cross Words – Week 11 - WAY

Which Way are you headed?

- ❖ As with HOLY and OBEY, Are you yielding your life to God?

- ❖ Have you acknowledged that Jesus is the <u>only</u> WAY?

- ❖ This week, Yield your life to Jesus in all that you do. He is a loving Master who cares for His people.

PRAYER

Father, I thank You that as I Walk Always Yielding to Your perfect Will, I will find true happiness and PEACE. My life is not my own, I belong to you, thus I shall yield my life to you. I know that there are times where I insist on my own way, yet I know that way only leads to destruction -- Your WAY always gives life. Amen.

Cross Words – Week 11 - PRAISE

PRAISE

Proclaiming **R**ighteous **A**cclamation **I**nspiring **S**omeone's **E**xcellence

Psalm 26:7;

> [7] *proclaiming* aloud your *praise*
> and telling of all your wonderful deeds.

Proverbs 27:2;

> [2] Let another *praise* you, and not your own mouth;
> someone else, and not your own lips.

When you praise someone, you are proclaiming that this person is excellent and should be acknowledged with high regards. We praise someone for the good work they have done. We praise someone for their consideration. We praise someone for complying with the standard (work, home, church). Yet, isn't amazing that we can praise someone one moment and then say hurtful things to them the next. Scripture speaks directly of this.

James 3:10-12;

> [10] Out of the same mouth come *praise* and cursing. My brothers, this should not be. [11] Can both fresh water and salt water flow from the same spring? [12] My brothers, can a fig tree bear olives, or a grapevine bear figs? Neither can a salt spring produce fresh water.

Cross Words – Week 11 - PRAISE

The perfect example is that of how we should praise God; He is the very essence of excellence and when we praise Him we are in fact proclaiming to the world and Him with righteous acclamation (words of praise) that He alone is worthy. Now, does God need to be inspired? No. But, He created us to praise Him and to develop a wonderful relationship with us. The more we praise Him, the less our problems have strength over us. Worship is the highest level of praise, and only God deserves this.

Philippians 1:9-11;

> [9] *And this is my prayer: that your love may abound more and more in knowledge and depth of insight,* [10] *so that you may be able to discern what is best and may be pure and blameless until the day of Christ,* [11] *filled with the fruit of righteousness that comes through Jesus Christ--to the glory and praise of God.*

The song that has been named the "Doxology" has always given me great elation and it reminds me who is in control of the things of this life.

Doxology

Praise God from whom all blessings flow

Praise Him all creatures here below,

Praise Him above ye Heavenly Host,

Praise Father, Son, and Holy Ghost. Amen.

Cross Words – Week 11 - PRAISE

- ❖ Praise God for everything.

- ❖ Praise your friends and family everyday.
  - o When you do, you are inspiring them to keep doing the excellent things they do.

- ❖ Praise and Worship is essential in our life. Find music and/or a place of Worship that focuses on Praising God.

PRAYER

Father, I PRAISE and thank You for all the wondrous things you've done, both in this world and in my life. You are the essence of excellence. I desire to make my life a PRAISE offering unto you. Help me to PRAISE others, rather than curse them. Amen.

Week 12

CHURCH

What purpose does it serve?

CHURCH –

Come **H**ave **U**nderstanding **R**egarding **C**hrist's **H**oliness

ALTAR – **A**llows **L**ives **T**o **A**cquire **R**edemption

PASTOR –**P**repare **A**nother **S**oul **T**o **O**btain **R**edemption

RNR – **R**elationship **N**ot **R**eligion
(not my own -author unknown)

Cross Words – Week 12 - CHURCH

CHURCH

Come **H**ave **U**nderstanding **R**egarding **C**hrist's **H**oliness

Matthew 16:18
> .....*on this rock I will build my <u>church</u>, and the gates of Hades will not overcome it.*

By going to a church, you will be assisted with your new growth, (What athlete can show up for game day without first practicing with the team first?), and be able to complete Christ's request, that you be baptized. Keep in mind, going to church doesn't save you either, developing a relationship with our Lord does. Going to a **CHURCH** that encourages you, challenges you, and feeds you with the Word of God does guide you on the right path in your relationship with Him.

The **CHURCH** you go to should have a similar spiritual focus as your own, encourage and strengthen you, and enable you on your walk with Jesus. It is better to be a contented Christian than a miserable Man (or woman). Wherever your place of worship is, find ways to grow in your relationship with Jesus, and help encourage those who are members of the body there.

Cross Words – Week 12 - CHURCH

When Christ comes again, he will not be coming just to the Pentecostals, or just Baptists, or just Catholics, etc., He will come for all true believers, whatever their type of church is; as long as they preach and live out their faith in Him.

I was talking to a friend of mine, one I hadn't seen in years, who is a currently a college student, and felt it unnecessary to belong to a church to have faith.
I told her, " Yes, this is true."
Then I asked her, "You could just take accredited college courses over the Internet right?"
She said, "Well, yeah, but I need to have the instructions explained to me, and I need to have others around me to motivate me."
Then I exclaimed, "That's exactly what I am talking about! We need God's instructions explained to us and we also need each other for support and motivation."

I heard it said that a CHURCH is a hospital for the sinner, not a spa for the righteous. What are we doing to bring healing to those that come to our CHURCH? We are the body of Christ, embodied here on earth; so it is through true Christians who are a part of the body of Christ that sinners can find Jesus.

Cross Words – Week 12 - CHURCH

- Have you found a **CHURCH** that feeds and encourages you?

- Remember, to **H**ave the **U**nderstanding of **C**hrist, you must first **C**ome, and **C**ome just as you are.

- Some people are bothered by all the "hypocrites" in the **CHURCH**, but at least they are coming to have better Understanding about Christ and how to be better.

PRAYER

Father, please bless your CHURCH. I am thankful for the ability to have a place where I can come to understand who Christ is. Help me to find and remain in a CHURCH that honors you. As I attend, help me to find ways to build up the CHURCH. Amen.

Cross Words – Week 12 - ALTAR

<u>ALTAR</u>

Allows **L**ives **T**o **A**cquire **R**edemption

Psalm 43:4;

> *"Then will I go to the <u>altar</u> of God, to God, my joy and my delight. I will praise you with the harp, O God, my God."*

Many times in Scripture, people would put up ceremonial stones stacked on top of each other in the form of an altar. This was most likely done to remind them, whenever they passed by it, that this was a place where God spoke to them or had a significant experience with God.

The altar of God, in most Christian churches, does allow for people to come forward to acquire redemption. Though people can receive redemption outside of the altar, it does allow for people to see their need and come before a leader of their church and receive God's grace.

Some churches have a term called an "Altar call", this is where people are encouraged to come forward and asked to be prayed

Cross Words – Week 12 - ALTAR

over to receive the gift of salvation in their life. Coming to the altar is just the beginning, it is up to the Christians around them to continually feed and lead the new follower.

Once you have accepted Jesus as your Lord and Savior, remember to mark that date forever in your memory, because Satan will try to steal this belief from you.

So, when Satan tries to tell you, "You're not a Christian, you're not going to have eternal life!" just respond with, "I know I am a sinner, saved by Christ's Blood, and I gave my heart to Jesus on _(date of dedication of your life to Jesus)_!" Have you ever tried to return something to a department store without a receipt? The store wants some proof that you actually purchased something there, and our Decision date is like that receipt; it reminds us, and Satan, that we have been purchased by the Blood of Jesus.

Romans 10:9-13;

> [9] *That if you confess with your mouth, "Jesus is Lord," and believe in your heart that God raised him from the dead, you will be saved.* [10] *For it is with your heart that you believe and are justified, and it is with your mouth that you confess and are saved.* [11] *As the Scripture says, "Anyone who trusts in him will never be put to shame."* [12]

Cross Words – Week 12 - ALTAR

> *For there is no difference between Jew and Gentile--the same Lord is Lord of all and richly blesses all who call on him, [13] for, "Everyone who calls on the name of the Lord will be saved."*

It is important to remember that you cannot earn salvation; rather, it is a free gift of God through grace. If someone were to offer you a million dollars, how would you react? Would you wonder what they wanted or were up to? Would you want to do something in return thinking that it would be the only way to repay them? But if the giver says, "I merely want you to receive this gift, no obligations or requirements. All I want is to be your friend." Don't you think you would be overwhelmed with gratitude and love? That is how the gift of Salvation is.

Ephesians 2:8-10;

> [8] *"For it is by grace you have been saved, through faith-- and this not from yourselves, it is the gift of God--* [9] *not by works, so that no one can boast.* [10] *For we are God's workmanship, created in Christ Jesus to do good works, which God prepared in advance for us to do."*

Do you believe in Jesus Christ? That He died for your sins, and rose from the dead? Are you willing to trust Him with

Cross Words – Week 12 - ALTAR

your life, in the good times and the bad? Are you ready to take the first step of faith? Do you understand that Christ forgives everyone, no matter what the magnitude of his or her sin? If you answered yes to these questions, might I encourage you to take this moment in your life to give your heart and

mind over to Jesus by praying the "Sinner's prayer"? If so, please recite these words:

> *"Dear Jesus, I accept you as my Lord and Savior, I acknowledge that I am a sinner. Please forgive me. I understand that I need you to help me through the storms of my life. I now accept your gift of salvation, by faith, which you purchased for me upon the cross. Today, I choose to follow you for the rest of my life. And, I know that by faith I will grow stronger each day. Help me to show others of your saving grace. Thank you Jesus. Amen.*

Whether this was your first time or just a re-dedication of your life to Jesus, know that this is the beginning of the rest of your eternal life. Live each day for Jesus. Also know that the host

Cross Words – Week 12 - ALTAR

of heaven and Christians all over the world are rejoicing because of your salvation and will continue praying for you.

We may not know you by name, yet we will continually thank God for every new Christian that comes into the family of God.

- ❖ **In Romans 12: 1** ; it states

    "Present your bodies as a <u>living sacrifice</u>, holy and acceptable unto God"

- ❖ Have you come to the **ALTAR** to acquire Jesus' Redemptive power?

- ❖ Ask a church leader about the **ALTAR** at their/your church – how can you use the **ALTAR** to know the Lord better, and to bring the needs of others before Him?

PRAYER

Father, as I come before you at the ALTAR of grace, Allow me To Acquire Redemption. Thank you for the gift you gave through your precious Son's death on the cross then conquering death through the Resurrection. Help me each day to be as a living sacrifice unto you – giving up more of what I want and clinging to what you want for my life. Amen.

Cross Words – Week 12 - PASTOR

PASTOR

Prepare **A**nother **S**oul **T**o **O**btain **R**edemption

Ephesians 4:11-13;

> [11] *"It was he who gave some to be apostles, some to be prophets, some to be evangelists, and some to be pastors and teachers,* [12] *to prepare God's people for works of service, so that the body of Christ may be built up* [13] *until we all reach unity in the faith and in the knowledge of the Son of God and become mature, attaining to the whole measure of the fullness of Christ."*

Just as a professor's job is to prepare their students for their final exam, so too does a Pastor prepare his/her congregation for their final judgment. Like a professor, a Pastor can only present the information needed for the person to be prepared. However, it is up to the person to choose to study the information and apply it to their life. The professor was once a student, and had to develop wisdom and understanding to attain their position. Likewise, the Pastor was also once a member of a church, and had to learn the information before he/she could lead. The professor does not take the Final exam for the student, nor does a Pastor take the place for us on the Final Judgment.

Cross Words – Week 12 - PASTOR

Don't leave all the work around the church up to the Pastor; remember, his/her job is to prepare you for ministry. Consider how Jesus handled this with the disciples. He told them to go out and fish, while he slept in the boat. He was probably tired from preaching, thus the disciples had to do the work. Pastors should be able to concentrate on preparing God's people through preaching and encouragement, and not be stressed over every aspect of the church. Alleviate the load for them! As the Scripture above states, "some to be apostles, some to be prophets, some to be evangelists, and some to be pastors and teachers." Notice that the pastor is a part of the other roles, not the only role. Appreciate their role in the church and enable them to have the time and resources to do their job and spend time with their family.

- ❖ Are you a **PASTOR** that is **P**reparing **A**nother **S**oul **T**o **O**btain **R**edemption?

- ❖ Are you encouraging the **PASTOR** of your church?

- ❖ This week, as a **PASTOR**, decide how you can get the message across that you are really there to prepare each member or your church and motivate them to realize the redemptive grace God has for each of them.

Cross Words – Week 12 - PASTOR

❖ -- If you are not a **PASTOR**, this week, take time to help your **PASTOR**, and encourage them to see how much they are appreciated. Help them so that they have more time to help you.

PRAYER

Father, I thank You that you have called men and women to be PASTORs, to Prepare souls to obtain Your redemptive grace. Strengthen them and guide them in all that they do. Help us to come alongside them and lift their spirits when they are down and alleviate some of the load. I pray you protect them from the power of the evil one who wants nothing more than to see them fail. By the power of Jesus Christ, who first established the church and designed for PASTORs to lead their congregation. Amen.

Cross Words – Week 12 - RNR

RNR

Relationship Not Religion

Many of us recall that RNR used to stand for "Rest N Relaxation", but a man I know, Ben, shared with me that he had heard it as **R**elationship **N**ot **R**eligion. Religion is man's way for reconciling Himself with God, Christianity (which requires a personal relationship), is God's way of reconciling Himself with man. When religion isn't the reason for believing, you will also get rest and relaxation.

Romans 2:17-24;

> [17] Now you, if you call yourself a Jew; if you rely on the law and brag about your <u>relationship</u> to God; [18] if you know his will and approve of what is superior because you are instructed by the law; [19] if you are convinced that you are a guide for the blind, a light for those who are in the dark, [20] an instructor of the foolish, a teacher of infants, because you have in the law the embodiment of knowledge and truth-- [21] you, then, who teach others, do you not teach yourself? You who preach against stealing, do you steal? [22] You who say that people should not commit adultery, do you commit adultery? You who abhor idols, do you rob temples? [23] You who brag about the law, do you dishonor God by breaking the law? [24] As it is written: "God's name is blasphemed among the Gentiles because of you."

Cross Words – Week 12 - RNR

It is sad that some people only "go through the motions" when they go to church; they say and do everything they should, but don't put their whole heart into it, all week long. A friend of mine told me about another interesting story that explains this issue.

Imagine that you are to go to the hospital for surgery. As you are in the Operating Room, lying there on the gurney, your family is able to watch through the glass. The doctor begins the surgery, and as she starts, your family notices that it looks as though she is giving you anesthesia, after all she did put the mask on your face. Then it appears as though she is making an incision with a scalpel to open the area. She moves her hands as though she was repairing your heart, and finally, acts as though she is sewing you up. With a smile, she says to your family, "All done, everything went well!" and sends you home that very day. However, when you get home, you notice that there is no incision, and you still ache from heart stress. Why? The doctor appeared to do all the right motions, but did not actually get to the heart of the problem – actually working on the heart.

Cross Words – Week 12 - RNR

- ❖ Do you have a Relationship with God, and not just the motions of Religion?

- ❖ Do you want to experience true happiness and joy through a great Relationship with God?

- ❖ This week, focus on your Relationship with God. What could you do to better this relationship?

PRAYER

Father, I praise and thank You for allowing me to have a personal Relationship with You. I pray that I do not get caught up in the ways of Religion, rather that I come to know you and love you through this wonderful Relationship. I know I will have Rest N Relaxation when this happens. Amen.

Week 13

<u>ANGELS</u>

Who's looking out for you?

ANGELS – **A**lways **N**ear **G**uarding **E**very **L**iving **S**oul

ACTS – **A**lways **C**onsider **T**he **S**pirit

BRAVE – **B**old **R**esilience **A**nd **V**aliant **E**ffort

MUSIC – **M**ake **U**plifting **S**ongs **I**nspiring **C**hange

Cross Words – Week 13 - ANGELS

ANGELS

Always Near Guarding Every Living Soul

Psalm 91:11,12;

*[11] For he will command his angels concerning you
to guard you in all your ways;*

*[12] they will lift you up in their hands,
so that you will not strike your foot against a stone.*

When I first received the word it was ANGEL – Always Near Guarding Every Life, and I thought that it had come from the Lord. He tells me that I had almost got it right, however, the angels do not guard the life of a cockroach, and He believed it best to add the S as to show the multitude and magnitude of the ANGELS and also to show that the ANGELS guard living souls not just any life.

Many people are amazed by the wonder and beauty of angels, and it is right to give them respect. However, when you put them above the One who created and sent them, we miss the point of their being. Besides, we will, when we are in Heaven, judge the angels.

Cross Words – Week 13 - ANGELS

1 Corinthians 6:3;

"Do you not know that we will judge angels? How much more the things of this life!"

- Do you love **ANGELS**?
    - - If so, what is it that you love about them?
- Do you feel you need their Guardianship?
- Do you realize that there good and bad **ANGELS**? Obviously the bad ones do not want to Guard Living Souls, rather to ruin them. God's Angels are there to protect His people.

PRAYER

Father, thank you for creating your magnificent ANGELS that are here to Guard and protect me. I appreciate them, yet I remember that it was you who created them. Keep them ever near to me today, to protect me from the power of the evil one. Amen.

Cross Words --Week 13 - ACTS

ACTS
Always Consider The Spirit

Acts 16:7;
> *7 When they came to the border of Mysia, they tried to enter Bithynia, but the Spirit of Jesus would not allow them to.*

Many times, throughout Scripture, especially in the Book of Acts of the Apostles, the Holy Spirit would either cause someone to go a certain way or not. When we consider the Spirit, we are more likely to see God's plan work according to His design. Sure, the disciples could have decided to go anyway, but who knows if they would have been able to reach people there, or worse yet, be killed because they didn't heed the Spirit.

Only second to God's saving gift of Salvation through Jesus' willing death on the cross, is the Spirit of God. He knew that we would struggle and have our doubts and misunderstandings, so Jesus said that He would send us a Paraclete or "helper".

Cross Words -- Week 13 - ACTS

Having the Holy Spirit in your life to lead and guide you is essential to our walk with Jesus. I know many times when I have been confused about a certain passage of Scripture or a situation, the Holy Spirit has gently been my counselor, teacher, and friend to help me through.

Are you struggling with what you read in Scripture? Learn from the One who wrote it. He wants nothing more than to explain the exact intention He has behind that particular Scripture.

"Come Holy Spirit, come"

- ❖ Take time this week to Consider The Spirit in all that you do.
- ❖ ACTS has also been used to help us understand how to pray:
    - A – Acknowledge God and His majesty
    - C – Confess your sins to God through Jesus
    - T – Thank God for everything in your life
    - S – Supplication – ask God to provide for you the things you need

Cross Words -- Week 13 - ACTS

PRAYER

Jesus, thank you sending the gift of your Holy Spirit. Help me Always Consider The Spirit in all that I do. Lead me, guide me, Holy Spirit on the direction the Father has for me. Help me to consider more of your ways and less of my own. Be near to me everyday, as I know I need you. Teach me the meaning of God's Holy Word, please. Amen

Cross Words -- Week 13 - BRAVE

BRAVE
Bold **R**esilience **A**nd **V**aliant **E**ffort

2 Samuel 13:28;
> *Don't be afraid. Have not I given you this order? Be strong and <u>brave</u>."*

The conclusion to our National Anthem says, "For the land of the free, and the home of the BRAVE." We have some of the bravest men and women in the military and rescue workers in the world.

We know of a man that gave his life to rescue trillions (all the people who ever lived) in one day from the eternal fire, and yet, He has still not been recognized as a "National Hero". He did it all, not for fame and recognition, but rather, to rescue each and every person, that is willing to acknowledge this great feat that He has done for them, to rescue them from Satan's grasp.

He carried upon Himself, the sin of the whole world, past,

Cross Words -- Week 13 - BRAVE

present, and future, a weight that is far greater than the physical weight of our world. He was the real Atlas, to carry the world on His shoulders!

Just as a firefighter must wear special gear to enter into the flames, so too did Jesus. He had to be pure, without sin, and yet, carry sin upon him. He had to sacrifice His own life, willingly, so that we might have life.

Jesus says in **John 15:13;**

> *"Greater love has no one than this, that he lay down his life for his friends."*

He paid the price for all of us.

❖ What situations in your life require you to be BRAVE?

❖ If you know someone who is in the military or in services such as a police officer, rescue worker, or fireman, be sure to tell them how much you appreciate their BRAVEry.

Cross Words -- Week 13 - BRAVE

PRAYER

Father, thank you so much for the men and women who have given their lives to save others, protect those who are still out there helping others through being BRAVE. Give me a Bold Resilience And a Valiant Effort to help others and to fight off the enemy's attacks. I know that "[12] our struggle is not against flesh and blood, but against the rulers, against the authorities, against the powers of this dark world and against the spiritual forces of evil in the heavenly realms. [13] Therefore put on the full armor of God, so that when the day of evil comes, you may be able to stand your ground, and after you have done everything, to stand." - (Ephesians 6-12,13). I can do all things, through Christ who strengthens me. Amen.

MUSIC

Make Uplifting Songs Inspiring Change

Ephesians 5:19,20;
[19] Speak to one another with psalms, hymns and spiritual songs. Sing and make <u>music</u> in your heart to the Lord, [20] always giving thanks to God the Father for everything, in the name of our Lord Jesus Christ.

Keep in mind, **MUSIC** isn't **MUSIC** unless it is both Uplifting and Inspires Change, otherwise it is merely noise. God communicates with us through **MUSIC**.

I have always enjoyed various types of **MUSIC**, and it has changed for me throughout the years: when I was younger, I enjoyed the popular 70s and 80s music. I even fell into the "Heavy Metal" and Hard rock era. Then I found myself trying out classical and various Christian artists. Some actually inspired me to change areas in my life. Now, I enjoy occasionally listening to classical, but, for the most part, I keep on Christian music (radio, CDs, tapes, etc.) on almost all the time. Above all, I love to spend time with worship music, which gives Honor and Glory that only God deserves.

Cross Words -- Week 13 - MUSIC

There have been numerous times when I have felt down or just in need of a word spoken from God, and that is when I just happen to turn on the radio and the exact right song comes on speaking directly to me in for that particular need or situation.

There is a song by Chris Rice called *"The Other Side Of The Radio"*, and in it he talks about his purpose for writing songs - to see a smile on someone's face. The song states what people go through while listening to songs on the radio - singing out loud, tapping their fingers, and bobbing their head. Chris has a way of writing songs that are uplifting and inspiring.

- ❖ Are you one who writes **MUSIC**? Consider the meaning, and find ways to Inspire others.

- ❖ When you listen to **MUSIC** – Does it truly Inspire you to Change?

- ❖ This week, choose to listen only to **MUSIC** that is **U**plifting and **I**nspires you to **C**hange for the better.

Cross Words -- Week 13 - MUSIC

PRAYER

Father, I thank You for the gift of MUSIC. I pray that whether I write music or listen to it that it would be only that which is Uplifting and Inspiring. I know that there are other types of songs to listen to, but I know these are not necessarily the ones that You can speak to me through. Praise your name, Jesus. Amen.

Cross Words – OTHER INSPIRING WORDS

<u>Other Inspiring Words</u>

(that God gave me)

ADORE -- **A**lways **D**esire **O**ur **R**edeemer's **E**xcellence
BLESS – **B**y **L**etting **E**ncouragement **S**trengthen **S**omeone
BREAD –**B**y **R**emembering **E**ternal **A**tonement **D**aily
EDGE – **E**very **D**ay **G**et **E**vangelizing
FIRE – **F**aith **I**gnites **R**evival **E**verywhere
HATE – **H**aving **A** **T**erroristic **E**ffect
JUST – **J**esus' **U**nbiased **S**ystem **T**riumphs
KIND – **K**eep **I**ncreasing **N**ice **D**eeds
JOY – **J**esus **O**verwhelms **Y**ou
RACE – **R**un **A**nd **C**ontinue **E**nduring
READ – **R**eally **E**njoy **A**nother **D**iscovery
SALE – **S**ecure **A**nother **L**ead **E**veryday
WAIT – **W**hen **A**ll **I**s **T**imeless
WORRY -**W**aiting **O**n **R**eality **R**epulses **Y**ou
WRITE – **W**e **R**eflect **I**nward **T**ranscribing **E**verything

<u>Words that I had seen before that helped to inspire me:</u>
BIBLE – **B**asic **I**nstructions **B**efore **L**eaving **E**arth
GRACE -- **G**od's **R**ewards **A**t **C**hrist's **E**xpense
PUSH -- **P**ray **U**ntil **S**omething **H**appens
DOG – **D**epend **O**n **G**od (Cute one for kids)

Conclusion

How do I apply these tools in my life?

Have you ever bought a new tool and when you took it out of the box you had no idea how to be put together? You may try for hours and hours, even then you may end up with left-over parts. These tools (the acronyms) can be valuable tools to encourage you everyday, and to provide wonderful tools for witnessing.

Let's compare two different procedures of witnessing: Like a Harrier jet (it takes off straight up with no need for a runway), and a small, single-engine plane. Sometimes, we approach people with, "Are you saved?!", which can turn people off because there was little to no preparation or fellowship time. This is most like the Harrier. We tend to want to get them in the jet quick, and then take off.

I have found great success, using these "tools" with the small plane approach.

1. First you must meet the people from the place they are at:

Cross Words – CONCLUSION

  --all people have a story, and there is a good reason why.
  --To merely tell them our story does not necessarily connect with them.

2. Slowly taxi down the runway, until it is the right time to prepare for take-off
  --Gently and lovingly get to know them
  --Let them know that you truly care about them
    --It has been said, "People don't care how much you know, until they know how much you care."
  --Give them reason to trust you.

3. Reassure them of your experience
  --Share your story with them
    --people can argue intellectually, but who can argue with a changed life?
  --Your story should reflect your life before you met Jesus, what brought you to the point that you realized you needed Him, and how has He changed your life?

4. After you have the "go ahead", begin down the runway
  --Start walking them through Scriptures.

Cross Words – CONCLUSION

--Ask them if they want to ask Jesus into their heart.

Revelation 3:20;

> *"Here I am! I stand at the door and knock. If anyone hears my voice and opens the door, I will come in and eat with him, and he with me."*

This is a clear and concise point that Jesus wants us to ask Him to come into our hearts! If you have ever seen the picture of Jesus knocking, you'll notice that there is no door knob on the outside. It must be opened from within! Once we open the door to our heart to Jesus, we will enjoy a wonderful time of fellowship at the table together.

Have you ever been invited to a wonderful dinner gathering? The meal and the table have been perfectly prepared, and the host is glad to see you. You feel special and honored when they put you in the best chair with the best food. Usually, all other matters can wait, because this is a time set aside just for you. That is the way we are to treat Jesus when He comes into our heart. What if the host brought out last week's leftovers? Would you feel honored then? Probably not! Why should Jesus get only what is "leftover" in our heart?

Cross Words – CONCLUSION

Galatians 2: 20-21;

> [20] *I have been crucified with Christ and I no longer live, but Christ lives in me. The life I live in the body, I live by faith in the Son of God, who loved me and gave himself for me.* [21] *I do not set aside the grace of God, for if righteousness could be gained through the law, Christ died for nothing!"*

The point I want to make is this: Jesus wants to come in and spend time with you, but you have to let Him in. Have you ever had someone come to your door and persistently knock or ring the doorbell, until you finally came? That is how much Jesus loves us! He will never give up! Won't you take the time from what you're doing with your troubled heart, and let Him in. Whenever Jesus went to the home of someone, even a sinner's home, He listened to them and encouraged them.

Many times, I have cleaned our house and thrown out things that I was "holding on to", things that I have not bothered to use or think about for years. This is exactly what Jesus wants to do in our heart, clean out the junk and fill it with joy.

I heard a rather funny story about a pastor that was visiting members of his church. He went to the door of one of the men

Cross Words – CONCLUSION

of the church, and rang the doorbell again and again. After some time, he left a note card with "Revelation 3:20" written on it. He didn't think too much of it until he received a note card in the offering plate that read: "Genesis 3:20". The pastor quickly found his Bible to recall the Scripture, *"He answered, "I heard you in the garden, and I was afraid because I was naked; so I hid."*

5. After you have the permission, take off with it!
   --The joy of knowing that another soul has been saved is exhilarating.
   --Encourage them and keep supporting them.
   -Get them to join a church that fits their needs.

A friend of mine, Michael, was reminding me of the wonderful crown we will receive in heaven, and I agreed it will truly be wonderful to put on the "Crown of life" on my head. Yet he also told me that the crown will only be as beautiful as we choose to make it... the more souls we win for the Lord, the more jewels it will have on it. He said, "I want my crown to be so heavy that I have to fall face-down before Jesus." Wow! That is what I want as well.

Cross Words – CONCLUSION

Know that "faith is the assurance of things hoped for and the evidence of things unseen." It is by grace alone, through faith, that believing and trusting in His unfailing love will save us. It is not enough to just believe; even the demons and pagans do that! Or, in the words of Tug McGraw, a famous baseball player, "Ya Gotta Believe!" We must be willing to trust God at all times.

> *Seek not to*
> *Understand that you may believe*
> *but Believe that you may understand*
> St. Augustine

Merely having faith is not the answer either. We must share our faith with others, namely, giving of ourselves through our time, talents, and resources. This is putting our faith into action.

If you are hurting, physically, mentally, emotionally, or spiritually, allow Christ to touch your life right now to bring about a complete healing.

As you go through the various steps of faith, allow yourself to grow and learn as you go. Always strive to attain perfection in your faith. Life is not perfect, Jesus is, and if we abide in Him our faith will be.

Cross Words – CONCLUSION

Have Only Positive Expectations about your Heavenly Father who loves you, and life will seem so much clearer and better to you. <u>Wait</u> on the Lord and expect only the <u>best</u> from Him, for He CAREs for you.

It is by the Cross, an emblem of suffering and shame, that our Savior, Jesus Christ rescued us. He stood in our place so that sin and death cannot have mastery of us.

Joy is an expression of elation, but it is also way to learn, through the tough times, how to persevere in our faith. When the tough times come upon you, know that <u>J</u>esus is <u>O</u>verwhelming <u>Y</u>ou with His love, compassion, and peace.

"No greater love has a man, than to lay down his life for a friend." Love one another. Hate only seeks to destroy, like a terrorist! Find ways to value everyone you meet.
Praise be to God our Father, to his Son, Jesus Christ, and to the Holy Spirit, both now and forevermore.

Forever in Christ,
 Nick "AcroNick" Furey

BIBLIOGRAPHY

Preface
2000 Zane Publishing Inc and Merriam Webster.
    All Rights Reserved
Colossians 2:2-6

Introduction -   **page 11**
1 Chronicles 4:9,10
Matthew 13: 31,32
Matthew 18:3,4

HOME –   **page 16**
2 Peter 3:13

MOM –   **page 19**
MOPs International
Mops.org

DAD -   **page 22**
Mark 14:36
"I want to be just like you"
    Phillips, Craig, and Dean
    Used with permission
Psalm 68:5

CHILD –   **page 24**
Matthew 18:2-5
Matthew 18:6

FAITH –   **page 28**
Hebrews 11:1
Ephesians 2:8
Matthew 13:58
Mark 6:4-6
Matthew 7:24-27

Cross Words – BIBLIOGRAPHY

HOPE –   **page 31**
Job 11:18

 LOVE –   **page 35**
John 3:16
Gary Smalley
1 John 14:16-18
1 Corinthians 13:4-8
1 John 4:7-12
Romans 8:35-39
Deuteronomy 7:9
1 John 3:1
Deuteronomy 6:5
Love for a lifetime
   by Dr. James Dobson

PRAY –   **page 41**
Ephesians 3: 16-17
Jeremiah 29: 11-12
Matthew 6: 5-15

GOD –   **page 46**
Colossians 1: 16-20
Hebrews 11:6

JESUS –   **page 48**
John 14: 6

LORD –   **page 50**
1 Samuel 24: 15

AWE -   **page 52**
Job 25: 2

CROSS –   **page 56**
1 Timothy 1:15
Galatians 1: 3-5
1 Corinthians 9: 15
Romans 10: 9-10
John 18: 36
Matthew 8: 11

Cross Words – BIBLIOGRAPHY

SAVED -   **page 61**
Hebrews 10:39
Romans 10:9,13
Ephesians 4:30
Romans 6:3-11
1 Peter 1:3-9
Titus 3:4-7
1 John 5:13

PEACE -   **page 65**
Philippians 4:7
John 14:27

ROCK -   **page 68**
1 Corinthians 10:3,4
Matthew 7:24-27
2 Samuel 22:2-4

GROW -   **page 72**
2 Corinthians 10:15
Proverbs 8:11,12
Psalm 90:12
Proverbs 21:11
Acts 7:10
James 1:15

PURE -   **page 75**
Psalm 19:9,10
Psalm 119:9

CHOICE -   **page 78**
Acts 15:7-9
Joshua 24:15

HEAR -   **page 80**
Revelation 13:9
12 Seeds of Successful Relationships
  by Norm Andersen-River City Press

Cross Words – BIBLIOGRAPHY

FEAR -   page 84
Isaiah 43:1
Isaiah 54:14
Wolf Ridge Environmental Learning Center, Finland MN
Psalm 110:11

DOUBT -   page 88
Mark 11:23-24
Proverbs 3:5
James 1:6-8

GUILT -   page 90
Psalm 38:4
Isaiah 6:5-8
James 3:7-12
Philippians 4:8,9
Colossians 3:17

SHAME -   page 94
Isaiah 54:4
Romans 10:11
Hebrews 12:2,3
Proverbs 25:9,10

SIN -   page 98
1 John 2:12

STOP -   page 101
1 Peter 3:7
Isaiah 1:15

EVIL -   page 103
Matthew 6:13
Revelation 20:1-3;7,9-10

Cross Words – BIBLIOGRAPHY

LUST - **page 108**
1 John 2:16-17
James 4:7-8
Every Man's Battle –
    by Steve Arterburn and Fred Stoeker
Matthew 5:27-28
Genesis 2:24

HOLY - **page 116**
Jude 1:20-2
1 Peter 1:15-16

OBEY - **page 118**
Matthew 8:27
Colossians 3:20
Ephesians 6:1-3
"Trust and Obey"
    by John H. Sammis and Daniel B. Towner

WORD - **page 121**
John 1:14
Matthew 4:1-11
Hebrews 4:12
John 6:
John 3:16

ZEAL - **page 125**
Romans 12:11-13
Romans 10:2-4

CARE - **page 128**
John 21:16
Luke 10:30-37

SMILE - **page 132**
Job 9:27
1 John 3:18-20

Cross Words – BIBLIOGRAPHY

GIVE -   **page 134**
Romans 12:8
Deuteronomy 6:5
Mark 8:34-38
"Thank You" by Ray Boltz
Matthew 25:14-30

HUG -   **page 139**
Ecclesiastes 3:5
Hugs for the Hurting
Stories by John William Smith and Personalized Scriptures by LeAnn Weiss
©1997 by Howard Publishing Co., Inc.

PAST -   **page 142**
Isaiah 43:18
"When the devil reminds you of your past, remind him of his future"--
Carmen
Matthew 11:30
"Give them all to Jesus" - Evie

PRIDE -   **page 145**
2 Corinthians 7:4
Proverbs 11:12
James 1:9-11

SORRY -   **page 148**
2 Corinthians 7:8-13

FORGIVE -   **page 150**
Matthew 6:12, 14-15
Psalm 79:9
Matthew 18: 21-22
Genesis 4:24

TRUTH -   **page 156**
John 14: 4-7
Proverbs 14: 12

Cross Words – BIBLIOGRAPHY

TRUST -   **page 159**
"Faith begins in the Wilderness"
   by Elizabeth Elliot
Proverbs 3: 5-6
1 Corinthians 2: 4-5
Lord Give Me Time – Author unknown

WAY -   **page 165**
John 14:4-7
Proverbs 14: 12

PRAISE -   **page 167**
Psalm 26:7
Proverbs 27: 2
James 3: 10-12
Philippians 1:9-11
"Doxology"

CHURCH -   **page 172**
Matthew 16: 18

ALTAR -   **page 175**
Psalm 43:4
Romans 10: 9-13
Ephesians 2: 8-10
Romans 12: 1

PASTOR -   **page 180**
Ephesians 4: 11-13

RNR –   **page 183**
(Author unknown)
Romans 2: 17-24

ANGELS -   **page 188**
Psalms 91: 11-12
1 Corinthians 6:3

ACTS -   **page 190**
Acts 16:7

Cross Words – BIBLIOGRAPHY

BRAVE - page 193
2 Samuel 13:28
John 15:13
Ephesians 6: 12-13

MUSIC - page 196
Ephesians 5: 19-20
"Other Side of the Radio" by Chris Rice

Conclusion - page 201
Revelation 3:20
Galatians 2: 20-21
"Ya Gotta Believe" –by Tug McGraw
St. Augustine

Cross Words – ILLUSTRATION

Here are some scriptures that were shared with me in an illustration:

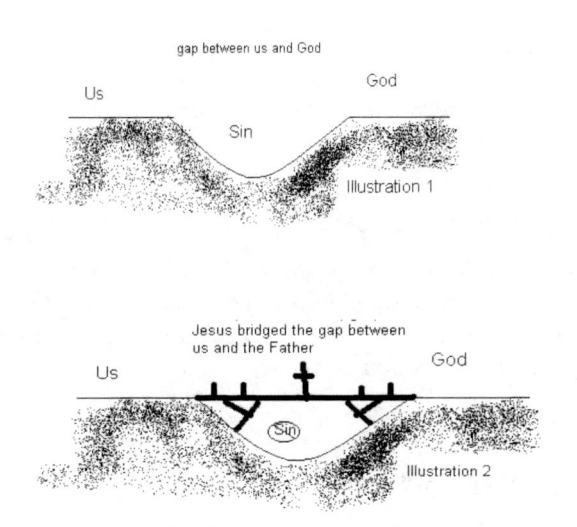

Illustration 1

Illustration 2

We had no way of approaching the Father, because of the huge abyss that separated us, due to sin (see illustration 1). And no matter how much we would have tried, it would have been impossible to crossover the abyss. The Father, out of His great love for us, sent His only, perfect Son, to take our sin upon Him, to lay down His life to bridge the gap for us. (see illustration 2) So now, we can approach the Heavenly Father with boldness. This was all shared with me years ago in a study, based on the illustrations above.

Cross Words – ILLUSTRATION

Sin a fact: Romans 3:23

²³ for all have sinned and fall short of the glory of God

Sin's penalty: Romans 6:23;

²³ For the wages of sin is death, but the gift of God is eternal life in Christ Jesus our Lord.

Judgment sure: Hebrew 9:27-28;

²⁷ Just as man is destined to die once, and after that to face judgment, ²⁸ so Christ was sacrificed once to take away the sins of many people; and he will appear a second time, not to bear sin, but to bring salvation to those who are waiting for him.

Christ died for sinners: Romans 5:8;

⁸ But God demonstrates his own love for us in this: While we were still sinners, Christ died for us.

The Gospel: 1 Corinthians 15:3-4;

³ For what I received I passed on to you as of first importance: that Christ died for our sins according to the Scriptures, ⁴ that he was buried, that he was raised on the third day according to the Scriptures.

Christ a free gift: Ephesians 2:8,9;

⁸ For it is by grace you have been saved, through faith--and this not from yourselves, it is the gift of God-- ⁹ not by works, so that no one can boast.

About the Author

Though Nick has endured numerous hardships and failures, he has relied on Christ to sustain him. Though alcohol, nicotine, drugs, and other debilitating behaviors ruled over his life years ago, through the Grace of God he has been rescued from those bondages. The journey that God led him on has been both challenging and amazing.

Nick is active with Youth and Adult activities and studies at his church. He is also the founder of Simple Faithworks. He is a motivational speaker and a Certified Toastmaster.

Witnessing to people on the street is the key vision for Nick. ***"The harvest is ready, though the workers are few."*** Matthew 9: 37

Nick was employed as a Funeral Director for 14 years, and had found that it was a great ministry during that time. He is currently involved in book distribution to local churches, and other sales.

Nick lives with his three children, Sam, Joseph, and Lydia.

Cross Words – ACKNOWLEDGMENTS

Acknowledgments

First and foremost, I want to thank my Lord and Savior for "Rescuing" me, and for speaking to me and loving me when I needed Him. As in the Mylon LeFevre Song, *"He died for me, I'll live for him"* I want nothing more than to live for Him in all that I do. His faithfulness and guidance have more than sustained me through life. By His grace, He entrusted me with this ministry to help others understand the Gospel in a unique and simplistic way. For it is by Him that I live, move, and have my being. I know He is ALIVE!

To Sara, (Sweet And Radiant Angel) for believing in me and having the gift of knowing that writing was one of my skills. You loved me through all of my ups and downs, even when, at times, those downs devastated you. You will forever hold a place in my heart.

To my three wonderful children; Sam (Smiles Are Magnificent), Joseph (Jesus Our Savior Encourages People's Hearts), and Lydia (Let Your Dedication Influence All), for their childlike faith and belief that God could use me. You have helped me to open my eyes to the heart of God through

Cross Words – ACKNOWLEDGMENTS

the heart of a child. You have put up with my extended conversations with the numerous people I have encountered. I love each of you.

To my parents and family for giving me a solid foundation in my faith, and for loving and supporting me over the years.

To the men of my "Friday Morning Bible Study", for encouraging me and for just being a sounding board. Your prayers and support have been awesome. You dubbed me with the nickname of **"AcroNick"**. Also, I want to thank the men of "My Brother's Keeper", you have been a great source of accountability for me – thanks!

To the many clergy in my area who have encouraged me and listened to me over the years, may God richly bless each of you. Special thank you to Fr. Petrich for initially encouraging me to write the book, and the numerous others for encouraging the use of all of the new "words".

Cross Words – ACKNOWLEDGMENTS

To Bill Downs, and the staff at my former work for giving me the time and ability to work on my book.

A special thanks to Dale L., John S., Nate and Pete N., Scott P., Bob Wolf, and Lyle and Amy Poster, for being such wonderful friends over the years. You have blessed me beyond what you will ever know. Thank you for believing in me and for being there through some of the toughest moments of my life.

I owe a lot to a woman named, Melissa, that gave me a holy "kick in the pants" to get the book completed. We finally got the horse before the cart!

Finally, thanks to all the wonderful feedback from the many youth that I have shared these words with – it was for you that I wrote this: to give you a simple understanding of who God is.

Cross Words –

<u>Notes</u>